Best wi

David Bassett.

Nov '94.

WHY DON'T YOU GET OFF AND WALK?

DAVID BASSETT

UNITED WRITERS
Cornwall

UNITED WRITERS PUBLICATIONS LTD
Ailsa, Castle Gate, Penzance, Cornwall.

British Library Cataloguing in Publication Data

A catalogue record for this book is
available from the British Library.

ISBN 1 85200 056 2

Printed in Great Britain by
United Writers Publications Ltd
Cornwall

For vélo

Chapter One

The company push-bike replaced the company car. The change had nothing to do with the finances of the local commercial radio station, Plymouth Sound, where I was the begetting programme controller, but with driving the gold coloured Renault into a hedge while drunk.

It was after regular Sunday morning tennis with an opponent whose wife had recently been to France on a shopping weekend – returning with many bottles of French drink. The crash happened at the end of May 1981, and the court case took place in mid-August when I was fined, endorsed, and banned from driving for eighteen months. I had been alone in the car, and have been thankful for that ever since. Neither was anyone else, or any other vehicle, involved.

My reputation, in our listening area of Plymouth and south east Cornwall at the time was controversial due to my on-air work which covered many local political, and social, hot potatoes. I was not universally popular; the blameworthy mishap provided a degree of welcome schadenfreude for some. There was much publicity, and impatient interest on the part of local newspapers to know the date of my court appearance.

At this, I pleaded guilty, and when invited to speak in mitigation said only that I apologised 'for inconvenience caused'. I sensed a touch of disappointment in the court-room that there was nothing more. The magistrates and others had settled back, anticipating a bit of a show on the lines of 'It will be difficult, if not impossible, to serve the listening public unless I can drive.' After the Chairman

7

of the Bench had delivered the sentence, I paid the fine, handed over my driving licence, and at the front door of the building was met by reporters from both local and national media. There was a particular reason for this enthusiasm. As the court usher put it, "There's more interest in this case than in the last two murders we've had here."

This was not surprising. A few years beforehand, and as a contribution to the cause of road safety and the drink drive campaign, we and the police had done two programmes on the subject. In the first part I was the offending motorist, drinking about ten measures of real whisky, while the police and their doctor demonstrated with real breathalysers and needles, the bag blowing and blood drawing procedures. In the second episode, the forensic results were dealt with and explained. The idea made a strong impact in our own patch and nationwide. The *Daily Mirror's* headline was 'HERE IS THE BOOZE'. Unsurprisingly, the standard question to me thereafter was "What would you do if you were ever done properly for this yourself?" The thought was such an incubus, that I rejected the possibility. Now that it had happened, I found a couple of answers.

The first was to make a vow that if I ever did drive again, not a thimbleful of the weakest shandy would I drink; the second was to use the case as a short broadcast feature for the next Christmas and New Year season. I asked a JP (a fellow director of the radio station) to record the text of the sentence I had received. This was followed by my own brief speech. "Those words were addressed to me in August 1981. May they never be addressed to you." As a drink drive deterrent, this item, aired with intense frequency in the run up to the holidays, was no less effective than the drinking shows had been. Perhaps the motive's purity had been misunderstood by one constable who said, "We always thought you'd turn it to your advantage."

In 1981 there was no compulsory seat-belt legislation, and I had never fastened mine. I had not clunked, neither had I ever clicked. In the crash, my head had gone through the windscreen, and a lot of shattered glass was buried in my face. Ribs were either bruised or broken, struck against the steering-wheel. I regained a drunken consciousness in a

8

casualty ward at Freedom Fields hospital in Plymouth.

An ambulance crew had rescued me from the wrecked car, the accident having caused a serious traffic jam in the Sunday afternoon homeward bound rush hour on the Dartmoor road near the village of Roborough. Blearily I looked at my blood-soaked track suit, and saw three people — a nurse and two police officers, one of them a sergeant. Somehow I forced enough statutory air into the breath testing apparatus, and then felt the blood needle in my arm drilling and aspirating for evidence. Words being spoken were hazily familiar. It was a replay of what we had done on the air. But in the broadcast there had been no accident, and we were at an imaginary roadside. Here, we were in the nightmare of the real thing and I could think only of the wretched question beginning, "What would you do if . . . "

When the police left, a doctor and the nurse worked with tweezers, removing as much glass as they could, stitching as they went. Then there were X-rays seeking broken bones, rib cage strapping, and a few days' stay in the hospital before returning home for a week of wound licking. When all the dozens of stitches were plucked out, I walked with a permanent scar on the right side of my face which has caught the attention and interest of more than one German. "Were you at Heidelberg?" they ask.

The executive perquisite was a write-off, and on getting back to work (and before the court case) I was provided with a used Marina to drive before the inevitable ban. Then I took charge of the second bicycle in my life: it was a lightish blue three-speed tourer. The first had been a gearless Hercules which, during school holidays, I had ridden and lived for in south Devon and Bournemouth. All the youthful joys of cycling rushed back when I boarded the company push-bike for the first time. Arriving at the radio station in a lather after beating hilly Alma Road, I looked forward to the run home, and to all the rides to come.

In September 1982, I left Plymouth Sound as a director and its programme controller. The shareholders allowed me to take the firm's vehicle with me so that I was no longer merely its keeper, but the new and grateful owner.

About a year later, and as a consequence of careless

parking, a thief took it. The bicycle was not found. By this time the BBC had invited me to conduct a talk show called 'Afternoon Sou'West' with listeners' calls on the telephone open line as the chief ingredient. My wife had for some years been the principal family car driver, and in any case the BBC premises were only a twelve minute walk away from home, so that neither car nor cycle was needed for daily travel to work.

In 1984 I was planning to buy a replacement bicycle in time for the summer holiday. Early in the new year, however, I started losing weight rapidly. This pleased me very much, as having been born an efficient converter to fat, I have too easily carried beer bellies. Notch by notch, the trouser belt was drawn in. Colleagues and others tired of hearing the latest, tedious, waistline report. At the same time, there was an increasingly painful abdominal throb. It was hard to ignore, but at no time did I connect it with the weight loss. I found that by taking the maximum daily dosage of twelve aspirin tablets, I could dull the discomfort in the appendix region enough to work and sleep. Food was a diminishing interest. More and more often I was asked if I was all right. I was enjoying the effortless slim, and managing to live with the pile driving beats inside. My spirits kept up. If I allowed myself any anxiety, it was confined to believing that the trouble had to do with something like appendicitis or a harmless ulcer — and that given time, whatever it was would go away.

At the beginning of March I accepted that I should deceive myself no longer. The GP prodded the now flat stomach area for about fifteen seconds, and sent me urgently, immediately, for blood tests. I asked him what was wrong — it was an ulcer wasn't it? Or a faulty appendix?

"I don't know. All I know is that there's something not right in that tummy," came the reply.

This was all done in the morning, and I went to the studios as usual for 'Afternoon Sou'West' between one fifteen and three pm. I wondered if anyone would ask, on the air, how I was that day. Ritually, my reply was "Very fit. Thank you. Hope you are too." The enquiry came on that Monday — only once, but someone wanted to know the state of my health.

10

At Plymouth Sound, we had started a BUPA group membership scheme and after leaving, I continued paying the premium individually, and at a correspondingly higher rate. The GP knew this, and had taken various actions during the day about which I knew nothing. One thing he had arranged was an appointment with a consultant surgeon that evening at the Nuffield Hospital. At six o'clock the specialist was asking what he could do for me. An hour later, he said that he wanted me to have a barium X-ray in the morning. He agreed with the GP. There was 'certainly something not right with this tummy'. I was given a sachet of a violent purgative (Picolax) and told to eat and drink nothing more until after the barium examination. This started at nine the following morning, and for the second time in my life, the first having been the previous evening as part of the surgeon's investigations, I was thoroughly, medically, and scientifically buggered.

Before that, there had been tests for kidney trouble, chest, and lungs. It was good to be told later, "Your lungs are fine." I have been a heavy smoker since late teenage. The X-ray equipment dollied to and fro. After half an hour, I stopped thinking about the technology trespassing through my intestines, twisting and turning, backing and filling along the alimentary canal, and asked the expert how things were going.

"I think we're getting to the bottom of the problem," he replied confidently.

"That means the knife, I suppose?"

"Probably," said the radiologist. "The surgeon will tell you all about it."

The colon coursing, tumour seeking war-head probed and tunnelled on. I was an inner tube, so pumped up did I feel, with nowhere for the entrailed air to go.

At the end of it I ate a Mars bar, and went to the radio station to prepare for that day's show. I had said nothing about any of this to workplace associates. It was Tuesday, March sixth, nineteen eighty-four. It was a year for which I had built up a mysterious dread since reading Orwell's book of the same twelve months. Again, during the open line part of the programme, some listeners asked me how I was – only for the sake of pleasantry, and to get in a practice pot or two: to test a feel of the afternoon's conversational wicket. As always, I was, "Very fit, thank you."

Customarily, I went to the canteen after the post transmission clear up. On greeting her, the staff member behind the counter serving tea looked up, and glanced at me. She said nothing, and passed the teacup, saucer, and spoon. She was habitually jocular, and I fretted that I had unintentionally upset her. I had. Without realising it myself, I had started to look more toxic by the day. This lady had been away for over a week, and the colour change of my face had given her a shock.

By now, I was boring new holes almost daily in the wide buffalo hide trouser belts that I had bought during a decade of radio and television work in Montreal; and boring hearers as well, but only off the air. At the tea-table there was talk about Czechoslovakia with one of the film editors whose wife came from that country. He was describing the difficulties of obtaining the necessary visas and other documents when the family travelled to Bratislava, and when his mother-in-law visited them. Normally, I ignored the sound of the incessantly ringing canteen 'phone. On that afternoon, faking concentration during the chit-chat, I heard, painfully felt, every bell. Within two minutes, it tolled for me. I had to call the GP at once. He asked me to drop everything, and to go round as soon as possible. His surgery at the nearby health centre was an eight minute walk away, but that day it took me a quarter of an hour. I walked as fast as I could, knowing what his words would be.

"I'm afraid I have some very bad news for you, David."

We were both word perfect.

He told me that I had cancer of the colon. The intestine had been invaded by an aggressively large and growing malignant tumour, and the pain had been caused when it reached nerve endings. Next, he revealed that the tests had located as well, a potentially nasty polyp in the transverse colon. Presently that one was benign, but it too would have to go, more than likely in a second operation. The diagnosis was adeno carcinoma, and villus papilloma. The first I called Dracula, and the second, because it resembled

12

half an orange with fronds, Nell Gwynne.

On Thursday I was admitted to the Nuffield Hospital in readiness for surgery on the morning of Saturday, March the tenth. Plymouth Argyle had a good cup run in 1984, reaching the semi-finals in the FA competition when they were beaten by Watford. On the day of my first operation they played Derby at Home Park and drew one all. This was the first topic (after asking for ashtrays) that I raised at half-past five in the morning on the following Monday, when I came to consciousness again after the seven hour operation. Sunday, March eleventh, was an unlived, unknown day.

Following the surgical conquest of Dracula, I stayed in the hospital for a post operative period of twenty-three days, disconnected bit by bit from the many life supporting attachments that included food and drink pipelines, catheter, drain, and a bile disposal outlet. Unforgettable was the moment when the consultant took tissue in both hands and hauled this tubing free — out of a nostril, coiling it like garden hose.

The conqueror of Dracula and his theatre team had used a technique called right hemi-colectomy. About a foot and a half of the cancerous colon had been cut out, and the two ends joined together. I was saved by great skill, and favoured by good fortune to have come through this without need of colostomy bag, chemo or radio therapy treatment. The monstrous Dracula had been taken out. In one.

Eight weeks later, it was Nell Gwynne's turn. The same consultant surgeon told me that while he would make every effort to remove her via the scenic (anal) route, it might not be possible: in which case it would be necessary to have a temporary colostomy (this would mean a bag) or ileostomy, which would also go with a bag. I prayed hard that this potentially poxy gatecrashing thespienne would take her final bow and leave through the proper back stage exit. She did. As I came out of the anaesthetic, I heard the music of the Sister's voice, "It's over. Everything's all right. Scenic route. And so easy."

Two weeks later I left hospital having been allowed a bit of solid food only during the last two days. I was so skeletal by then that it actually hurt to have a bath — the hard tub surface pressed woundingly against bones shorn of all padding fat.

On Monday, June eleventh, nineteen eighty-four, I resumed work. The show had been well tended by others. It was good to be back, and to take on life again, although its priorities would, for me, never be the same.

Chapter Two

Four years later, I acquired my third bicycle — the vélo. It is a Raleigh Magnum: a mountain bike with fifteen dérailleur gears. Its colour is charcoal metallic, and it is fitted with ratchet thumb shifter gear levers. Soon after purchase, I put it aboard the ferry from Plymouth to Roscoff in northern Brittany to ride in France for the first time.

At the outset, my gear changing was bungled and botched. I would confuse the left and right hand controls, and frequently slipped the chain, not knowing what to do in these crises. I would then either wait for, or walk the powerless machine to expertise, when, after a few seconds, someone would deftly put things right.

During the next three years I rode around Brittany for spells in summer while fantasising on a great ride between Roscoff and Santander in northern Spain, from where we could take the ferry across the Bay of Biscay back to Plymouth. For this I would need the whole of June, July and August. I was able to arrange that with the BBC in 1991. Domestically, it was even easier.

Since our children came of age, my wife and I have, for many years, taken separate holidays. Although of cycling Dutch origin (and Canadian adoption) she prefers visiting family in Holland and eastern Canada to sharing my squalid vélo life style. We both enjoy our choices.

Serious cyclists consider the journey and distance between the ferry ports of Roscoff and Santander as a quite ordinary tour. Little or nothing to write home (or anywhere else) about. I asked an engineer at the radio station who is a proper cyclist, how long it would take him to ride from one to the other 'going downhill' from north to south. He looked at the atlas map I had shown him, and said, "About five days." And if racing? "About two and a half." I, however, was ill-trained, ill-equipped, and ill-prepared. At generous best I might be classified as a 'recreational' cyclist. Impractical, unpractical and mechanically useless, I had no tent because I cannot assemble one. Instead, a light sleeping-bag and bivouac have always had to do. A real cyclist, alone, or with others, would have almost no story to tell about this riding dare of my dreams. The account would be frustratingly brief: 'I put my bicycle on board at Plymouth, rode through France, turned right at the Spanish frontier, cycled up and down the Atlantic Pyrenees to Santander, and sailed back.'

On the last Friday in May 1991, I signed off the show, wished listeners a good summer, and promised to return on the first Monday in September. Then I rode home to pack the panniers for a midnight sailing to France.

Previously, on overseas trips with the vélo, I had ignored earnestly given, and experienced, advice about what, and what not, to carry. Sternly I was told, "One of everything on, and one of everything in the panniers. Only one spare. Absolutely nothing more. No need. Weight and space problems."

The prospect of having only two shirts, socks, and drawers to hand produced feelings of chronic insecurity: so at first I took half a dozen of everything with the result that the pannier bags were regularly full of filthy clothing. By the start of the big ride I had learned; and with the exception of handkerchiefs, the experts would have approved of our lean inventory. For footwear I had a pair of expensive, black, air-cushioned trainers for the main pedal work, tennis shoes, and flipflops. There was a wash bag and rechargeable electric razor.

The night was dark, wet and windy as we rode past the gaping bow doors. Above, the raised visor was open like a yawning parrot's beak. After I had seen the vélo safely lashed to a rail in the lower garage, I went on deck and shivered in the damp cold. The *Quiberon* moved out of Millbay Docks, turned, and headed into the sound. As we passed the break-water, I looked for somewhere to sleep. I had no cabin space, and dislike reclining seats, finding it impossible even to catnap on them. Anon, I would get the head down somehow.

I went to the stern and stood in a lee spot, and watched the lights of Plymouth and south east Cornwall merge to a loom, and in self challenge, questioned the sense of what I had set out to do.

In a crowded self-service restaurant I took a tray of tea to an emptying corner table, intending to lie under it after fellow passengers had left for cabins and reclining chairs. When the lights were dimmed, I stretched out, using the heavily zipped and multi-pocketed anorak as a pillow. This was my strongbox. In it were passport, tickets, wallet with French and English money and the precious plastic – Access and Visa cards. Keys, glasses, diary and tiny radio with miniature headphones were also stored and zip fastened away.

I settled foetally on the industrial carpet, and dozed fairly well. Suddenly, without warning or sound of any kind, something heavy struck my right foot. I looked up and saw two men walking off. One of them said "Sorry." The voice was English and I suspected that its owner had brought his foot down violently on mine, and not accidentally. The 'sorry' sounded bogus, but I could not be sure. Neither did my mood make me minded to establish guilt or innocence. Posteriorly, I turned the other cheek.

The *Quiberon* docked punctually at seven o'clock local time. We had lost an hour during the six-hour Channel crossing. After a tannoy announcement calling for drivers to report to their vehicles, I guided the well charged razor over my face assisted by a reflection from a curtained porthole on an upper deck. From past voyages I had found it better to wait until the motorised traffic had rolled off before doing so ourselves. Even after playing for time usefully, I found the companionways still crowded. Sleep starved eyes were red and filmy. The holidaymakers, many with pre-school children, struggled impatiently with bags and push-chairs in the narrow spaces. At the vélo I stashed the duty free whisky and rolling tobacco before unleashing the bicycle. The chain side was against me as I untied the securing rope and it stained my main pair of track suit

17

bottoms with large patches of lubricating oil from the liberal pouring I had given it before leaving home. I lectured myself testily about carelessness.

The noise in the cavernous garage was deafening. A throttling din of revving lorries, cars and motor caravans, mopeds and motor-bikes, reverberated echoingly and bounced around the ferry's hull. The stern doors opened, and muttering all the time, "ride on the right – ride on the right," we went over the ramp, past customs and immigration without stopping, and up the hill to traffic lights on a main road where we turned left. The weather remained unpleasant. The morning was grey and blustery with driving, passing showers. Even so, my spirits were high as in the manageable rolling countryside, I savoured the three, free, months to come. We set off and picked up a good rhythm. For some time we were overtaken with varying degrees of safety by the GB stream as the Britons legged it off the ferry, but after half an hour or so the vélo and I had the straightish roads and roundabouts (few and far between) mostly to ourselves. As on previous visits, I appreciated the good space given to cyclists by the majority of French car and lorry drivers. While hating each other, and disliking pedestrians, the French driver might prefer the journey on two, rather than four wheels. In the Fifth Republic the vélo is revered as La Petite Reine, The Little Queen, and is generally saluted.

My intention was to navigate to Santander by hugging the French and Spanish coasts: by keeping the sea, whenever possible, and sensible, to our right, consistent with steering a more or less straight course between points of departure. I had a map of Brittany which would guide us as far as Nantes – a place that may as well have been a moon town so distant did it look on that first morning of our long, adventurous journey.

The first destination was Landivisiau from where we would cut off the fat Brest promontory of Finisterre, and make southing via Sizun, Le Faou, Châteaulin, and eventually Quimper – another distant spot in space. We pushed on into the early morning wind and rain, with the stench of silage coming off the quiet land. Gradually I grew more confident about riding on the right, and was glad that the

18

roundabouts were conveniently empty at that hour.

Nevertheless I signalled vigorously to anyone interested in our intentions. The road sign pointings were confusing. Used to them being definitely angled at ninety degrees in Britain, it was difficult in strange terrain to know which way to go; and even after a good deal of practice, I was still not completely comfortable with the gear changes, and the first trouble came after an hour when we were eight kilometres out of Roscoff.

It was a bad blunder after taking a wrong roundabout exit. I realised that we were in the worst gear — too high for the incline — and hurriedly tried to correct, but made an awful hash of it, and then I was pedalling against nothing. Would I ever learn not to slip this essential metal linked, endless belt? I put the vélo on its stand, and tried to deal with the vexation myself. After a few cack-handed attempts, I gave up, and sat on the verge deciding, despite oil dark fingers, to roll a cigarette. Then, because of the steady rain and wind, I abandoned the smoke, put pouch and lighter away carefully in waterproof plastic, and tried again. This time, the vélo turned and looked at me from the front, as a horse will when not pleased with the treatment that it may be getting around its hind quarters.

Two minutes later a true, serious cyclist appeared (given time they always do) dressed, helmeted and riding as if in training for the Tour de France. In all ways, he was de rigueur. I hailed him, and spoke in my weak French. In under half a minute the chain was back in place, cog teeth ready to gnash and grind once more — until the next shambolic levering. We carried on in the wet.

At the top of the next hill there was a fork junction. In its cleft there was a solitary building in the lonely country-side displaying the red and white Kronenbourg sign. It looked like a farmhouse. I parked the vélo alongside the door. A few farmers were sipping early morning red wine served by Madame, a severe, matriarchal figure. I asked for café cognac and aroused a little interest. Nervous, I popped out every few minutes to view the vélo. After the third check-up, Madame, a bit out of humour at my concern, rebukingly assured me that there were no robbers in her vicinity. I relaxed, had some more café cognac, and joined in farming talk of which I understood little, but gathered that much of it had to do with the commune. Strengthened, we went on in the dismal weather, became more confident at handling the road conditions, and sustained by occasional breath and smoke stops, arrived in Landivisiau.

The town was oldish, clean and calm. It was time for more café cognac, and a submarine of a ham sandwich with mustard and butter. En route to our next stop, Sizun, we passed something like a block works. It billowed dust on the outskirts of Landivisiau, but I did not have even a speck of interest in whatever environmental damage this large plant was causing. My mission was to empty out my own dustbin of a head and to block, barricade, my mind against all but the most worthy thoughts. For three months I was determined to be done with the rubbish of life: all mental detritus (especially my own) would be seen off.

Although I had been told by the bicycle engineer in the shop where I had bought the vélo not to change gear if stationary, or to back-pedal, I next did that at a crossroads. Luckily we had enough momentum to get off the thoroughfare and on to side grass. I waited a few minutes for a genuine cyclist to appear, but only cars sped by us. There was no sign of a rescuer. We had already used up that day's quota of road knights. By now the rain had stopped, the wind was dropping, and there were signs of sun to come. I peered at the gearing and the chain and tried to work out how other human beings could do this easily, and probably with eyes closed. I had no gloves of any kind. The Tour de France champion, I had noticed, swapped his riding pair for oily ones he kept in a saddle-bag. Deciding to sacrifice a spare luggage plastic bag — there was no litter anywhere in sight — I wrestled clumsily in oil for about half an hour. It took that long to discover that by holding a springing arrangement, it was possible to get enough slack to slip the chain back onto the cog teeth.

Victorious, we carried on pedalling for some kilometres on flattish road, and then again a Kronenbourg sign came into view. It hung outside the door of another isolated farmhouse and was protected by half a dozen tethered, constantly barking dogs. I went through a narrow passage at the front of the house feeling like an intruder, relieved that the dogs were secure, and thinking that the beer advertising sign should have been removed years ago. In a small room on the right, a farmer was having a glass of red wine at the bar, and talking to ample Madame who was wearing a flower patterned print dress and ornate spectacles. Ignoring me for a short while, she went on with her dusting, immersed in the farmer's lot. He drank up and left, and had probably not been in for more than a few minutes. I had gathered from previous experience that here, customers do not stay for long drinking sessions. Little and often seems to be their way.

Madame, of middle years, looked at me and asked what I wanted — eyebrows raised quite high. Did she have beer on draught? Non. Then some vin rouge, please. We began a conversation, and she told me that she had been interviewed by the local radio station about a recent visit to Yugoslavia — her first travel out of France. Soon we were reminiscing over her school-days nearby, and she recalled a couple of English songs she had learned in childhood. Together we sang *My Bonnie Lies Over the O-see-er* and *It's a Long Way to Tipperary*. During the interval, I had a second, larger, glass of rough red wine, cleared the throat, and sang in duet with Madame, two French songs that I also remembered from school-days. We gave *Frère Jacques* and *Sur le Pont d'Avignon* a good belting. Madame sang like an angel, and we were on the most cordial terms when it was time to end our show.

About an hour later we arrived in Sizun, a place of some historic interest principally through its church, which we did not visit. Sight-seeing was not on our agenda; but lunch was, and I had some in a restaurant just off the Place (Town Square) where there could be found the usual crêperies, tabacs, boucheries, boulangeries, pharmacies, and pâtisseries. Over tasty moules marinières I ruled that vélo and I had done enough for day one, and that we would stay until next morning at 'Le Camping' on the outskirts, which I had seen signposted as we came in. Also, muscles of which I had not been aware before, started to ache and play up a bit.

The municipal campsite in Sizun was tidy and ordered. That was obvious even to me, though I had never been to one run by a local authority before. The weather, now in mid-afternoon, was much better. The sun shone and the temperature rose. The site was only about a third full. June is not a busy holiday month in France. There was no one in the office, but a friendly retired camper told me to help myself to a pitch. He, like all others when told, was astonished that I had no tent, with only sleeping-bag and bivouac for shelter and warmth o'nights. "No tent?" he asked repeatedly. Accustomed as I was to such typical reactions, the first questioning incredulity gave me increasing pleasure and amusement. Clearly, kind Monsieur could not wait to tell Madame, looking out from their well found caravan. Still worried about the safety of vélo (we were but a day and a half out of homeland), Monsieur said that he would guard it — parked under a tree close to a fast running brook — while I went on foot to the town for provisions.

Taking a short cut across a tiny bridge over the stream, I passed local women washing clothes in the rushing water, juxtaposing the incongruous computers I had seen in the campsite office. I bought baguette bread, cheeses, pâté and wine and looked forward to an alfresco dinner on the mini river-bank side. On its opposite shore was a newly mown hayfield, neatly baled. I wanted to walk in it, and reckoned that it would be easy to wade over in flipflops. Starting out, I took a painful purler as the current gripped the feet, and flipped off the left flop which sailed out at a high knot speed. It was lost forever. Putting on white tennis shoes, I tried and fell again, but slithering, traversed the few feet. Sopping wet, I finally established a beach-head in the hayfield. The fording in reverse was uneventful.

At six o'clock Madame appeared in the office, and I paid eighty pence for a night's lodging under the stars, or under dry or wet clouds. She was comforting on that point, asserting that there would be no rain this night.

With the camping knife and fork, but no plate, I tried to feed in the pleasant setting. I was joined by horseflies and mosquitoes who thought so much of me that they stayed all night when I tried to pass out inside the hot and stuffy sleeping-bag on slightly inclined ground. It was good to see the dawn. Red-eyed and bitten, I went early to the well equipped and designed sanitaire. I was uncomfortably stiff, and there was a pain in my saddle area. But I resolved to pedal through the achings.

Chapter Three

Gently, we rode and walked to Le Faou where we stayed for the first time in a gîte d'étape — a unique French idea combining the best and cheapest elements of youth hostels, with individual self-catering. In Le Faou the gîte was a dormitory with bunk beds on two floors connected by a spiral staircase. Madame, next door in the 'tourist information', admitted us and helped with the vélo — I remained paranoid about its security. It was not only my transport, but my address, and safety cache box as well.

Rather than carry the crucially valuable multi-purpose steed up the dangerously steep and narrow outside stairs, she suggested that we should ask for garaging in the nearby Priest's house, but I declined this offer. The vélo would have been out of sight, and the night, sleepless. Madame was long suffering and brave. Probably no other inmate in her experience had wanted to do this. We were both shaking at the end of the tricky, heavy lift. Reaching for breath, we sat down in the kitchen area inside, and I rolled cigarettes for us both. The return journey down, I predicted, would be even worse: I could not ask her again. A night's stay here came to twenty-five francs, about two pounds and fifty pence.

I had been in Le Faou before — in 1988. Sitting at an outside table on the terrace of the Café des Halles, I looked across the Place to the shell of a four centuries old building. It had been a crêperie — burned out by a friteuse (chip pan) fire. I was in the Café des Halles on a beautiful July evening of that year when it happened. The blaze beat eight teams of pompiers (firemen) who had rushed in from miles around.

24

There were no victims or injuries, but the town folk next morning, Sunday, walked sadly, as mourners go about the streets. On the night, I had just ordered dinner at a small window table in the upstairs restaurant, when the first flames tongued around the heritage rich house. We feeders had a perfect, grandstand from our places. Some rushed to the ground floor, but were swiftly returned by a gendarme.

Four hours after it had started, the conflagration finally won at midnight. Nothing was left but old, still smoking walls. Three years later, tidied up, the gutted, ancient and interesting edifice stood as I had last seen it — empty, and resting in peace. There were no other travellers (randonneurs) in the gîte d'étape and as the sole occupant, I had quiet sleep. In the morning, and dreading the descent with vélo, I decided to solicit help on the street, having put the bicycle on view at the top of the cliff-like stairway. Willing and strong passers-by took over, and in seconds we were back down to earth again, and ready for the off.

From the gîte d'étape booklet covering that part of Brittany, I saw that there was a facility on a farm not far away. We had travelled only a short distance but I especially wanted to pace and favour the hurting muscles. We would take it easy for the time being. This gîte was off the beaten track, and when we found it at the bottom of a steep valley, I saw sheep and donkeys but no sign of human life. The door of a dilapidated building opened onto a large stone floored room with a linoleum covered refectory-type table in the middle. I hauled the vélo up a few steps, and parked it inside, guessing that for the second night in a row, I could choose from any one of about thirty bunks.

Selecting a glass from an enormous wooden dresser, I took a bottle of ferry priced whisky to an outside barbecue table, and cogitated contentedly. Half an hour later, Monsieur appeared having just driven sheep into a field next to a pasture where donkeys grazed. Youngish and lightly-bearded, he was twinklingly pleasant, and we introduced ourselves. His welcome was warm and genial. He asked about food, and offered it. I said that I would like to eat at any time convenient to him and Madame. Taking the necessary items for the night out of the panniers, I chose a corner bunk in

25

b

the dormitory loft, clinging carefully to the single handrail on the constricted wooden steps.

I was about to snooze when the sound of English rose up from below. Monsieur was explaining things to Bob, a retired Englishman pedalling around Brittany for a month. We chatted briefly before he left on his much lighter, touring bicycle (a Raleigh Randonneur) to buy provisions for a self-catered meal. Too idle, and unable to do for myself, I felt no shame when he said that he would buy for me as well, in replying that I had arranged to dine à la maison. He laughed well at this, and I looked forward to more of his company.

Settling in the silence of a large, embattled armchair, I started what would have to be a longish happy hour. The Johnny Walker Red Label on the rocks was going down well, and helped me to think about the days, weeks, and months to come with the vélo. Surprisingly soon, Bob returned, and while scotch was not to his taste, our farmer host brought wine and we were quickly en fête. Monsieur fitted in visits between tending animals and dodging Madame. I suggested that she should join us. Monsieur grimaced and self-protectingly poured himself a greater measure from my bottle. We were all chummy, and full of entente cordiale.

Bob had been a boffin working on atomic energy. Although I had vowed to feed the fast emptying head with nothing but facile pleasure during my three month meander through Shangri La, I found his conversation and learning so easy to take, that by the time Monsieur brought grilled lamb chops to me, and Bob had laid out his cold meat collation, we had arrived at the prospect of individual nuclear pogo sticks and atomic powered bicycles for all. It was a convivial evening. Sleep came quickly, and lasted for seven unbroken hours.

In the morning and with mild hangovers, we went on our separate routes: Bob to the St. Malo ferry for the voyage home, I to Landevénnec, a picturesque village on an estuary at the bottom of a long, unsporting hill. As we rolled down at great speed, and well before arrival at water's edge, I was already dreading the return ascent.

Deciding to take a chambre in the area, I was given the key to what I thought was a room with en suite facilities. There was no plumbing, or extra door anywhere in sight. Thrice I

26

went to reception, and thrice with growing exasperation on both sides, I was told that in my room there was a lavabo, bidet, toilette and douche (shower) all ready for use; but where? I was on the point of inviting Madame to come up and show proof, when I saw an uneven bit of decorative paper on one wall. It was a sliding accordion arrangement which, when pulled aside, revealed a space with all the promised features.

Landevénnec is famous for its Benedictine Abbey ruins upon which much restoration work has been done over the years. From my cursory glance, it is a popular, frequently inspected site. Dinner that night was mainly local crustacean, but as usual I had embarrassing difficulty using the surgical instruments, and wastefully, left much of the succulent fruits de mer flesh inside the shells, able to tear away only some of the obstinate covering, protective to the end, when operated on by uneducated hands.

It was a tough climb up the long mountainous slope the next morning, but once at the apex we made good time on fairly flat, sometimes rolling roads to Crozon-Morgat, two adjoining towns administered by the same local authority. The weather was summery, and I wanted to spend a few days doing nothing by the sea. Morgat is a yachting centre: a pleasant, though commercial spot, with many hotels, cafés and ice-cream stalls.

I settled at a campsite, found a suitable tree-covered pitch, and shook out the sleeping-bag on rough grass. With the camping knife and fork, I made a light supper of ham, bread and pâté and tried to brew coffee with water boiled on a tiny spirit stove but had to throw it out. There was a strong taste of meths. I did not know (and cared little) what had gone wrong. Then some children arrived, and were gleefully astounded at my unusually primitive preparations for the night. They said that if it rained, I would have severe problems. It did, and they were right.

Mistakenly, I had thought that I would be completely waterproof wrapped inside my baggy cocoon. I tried to put the drenching out of mind, but soon the polo shirt and track suit trousers were moist. My immediate neighbours were a young German couple who had dined with elegant efficiency at a covered table outside their secure, tightly organised tent. When the rains came, they found reasons every now and then to look, agape, in my direction.

As night, and more rain fell, I gathered everything up, and went to the communal sanitaire to spend the night outside on the dry, sheltered, veranda-like area, by the laundry sinks. Noisy and drunk teenagers came and went until dawn, and held rowdy meetings inside. At seven I called it a night, did what I could with razor and toothpaste, and rode into the nearest town for breakfast.

When we were leaving, our German neighbour, tidy in his arrangements with shower coins and towel, passed by and talked. "Tell me," he asked in well spoken English, "do you always live like this, or only when you are on holiday?" A touch miffed at the impertinence, I replied, a little sharply, that this would be my chosen way of life if only circumstances allowed it. We left him shaking his head, willing, forcing, himself to believe that I actually did exist.

We set out for coffee and croissants and found a café open in Crozon near the town market and church. It was run by a kindly couple and their attractive daughter who showed exemplary understanding and sympathy when, in detail, I described the night just over. In the WC I saw that my eyes were blood red and heavy bagged. Monsieur was one of life's welcome optimists. He told me that the weather forecast was seasonally good. Feeling better and drier, heartened by their early morning company, and warmed by the sun, I rode to the nearest beach, planning to hang out the sodden sleeping-bag, and clothing, to dry.

A good idea came to me. I secured the vélo to a rock, and decorated it with as many wet things as I could safely tether to such a surprisingly natural clothes line. The conditions were perfect for the purpose: hot sun and strong off-sea wind. It was early June, there was plenty of room, and I had a good day lotus eating — reading, splashing about and watching the clothes and sleeping-bag blow dry.

The weather was on the change again when we got back to the campsite in the evening. Many Germans were busily trying to bring to the surface their submerged fleet of Mercedes Benz motor caravans. In command of the entire

28

operation was Gunnar, a school-teacher from the Ruhr. His subject was English. When the vehicles were on firm ground again, I congratulated him on his leadership, and said that he had reason to feel pleased, if not a little smug. He asked me for a precise definition of the word and wrote down my translation carefully in a notebook. I told him that he had earned his dinner and asked him what the menu was likely to be. He looked towards his own mobile home, and replied with some asperity, "Noodles."

I went to the office-cum-store, where after negotiating with the owning family, I was presented with the key to a kajibi — a tiny, head hurting, half gabled space adjoining the sanitaire block, but weather-proof and dry. Standing up in this Lilliputian potting shed was impossible: there was just enough height to move a step or so by stooping low. The lesson was harsh and painful. My head collided with the sharply cornered roof beam three times before I was careful.

Warily, I rearranged the spare rubbish bins, hosepipes, gardening tools and a couple of watering-cans, paint pots, rakes and brooms. There was now just enough space to lay out the wind-freshened, bone dry sleeping-bag.

I had some pâté, bread and cheeses, and named these quarters 'L'Appartement Royale' and drank to our future from a stainless steel cup full of sour red wine. When I told Monsieur and Madame and their four children, that I had bestowed the Royal Warrant, they were beside themselves with amusement, pleasure and pride.

Thunder and lightning started afterwards, but I felt so unbuttoned that I could have slept on nails, and probably was lying on a few, laid flat. The storm was violent. Soon the humidity was washed away by continuous, ferocious rain. At the peak of the tempest's roar I collapsed and slept.

Waking, I heard the deafening downpour, and saw by my watch that it was half past three in the morning. The wine had called me, and was pressing hard for release. I did not want another soaking by staggering to the sanitaire, and with the front light of the vélo (when detached it doubles as a torch) I found one of the watering-cans. This I intended

29

to use as a gesunder, or chamberpot. Later and in more moderate weather, I would empty the contents at leisure in the sanitaire.

Crouching on the unzipped, open sleeping-bag, I put the torch on the floor, and from this unfamiliar squatting position, held the watering-can with one hand, and aimed at it with the other. I could hear nothing, nary a tinkle, as the rainstorm machine gunned the building, but the relief on an overflowing bladder came quickly and was blessed. At the time, it did not occur to me that the watering-can should have weighed more. I was concerned only to be careful, and not to spill a drop, and held it with rock-like steadiness.

Clutching the vessel with both hands, I groped my way to what I hoped was a flat and safe surface near the door, gently lowered it, and crawled back. I started to zip up the sleeping-bag, and then found that I had drained myself upon the fleece. In dismay, I rolled it up, and lay on the dusty floor waiting for dawn's light. When it came, I saw that the rusty watering-can's bottom was holed in several places. Unseen by torch light, it could spray from either end. Not only would the sleeping-bag have to be dried again, but thoroughly washed as well. I doused and soaped it in one of the laundry sinks (they were deep and wide) and dried it on the same beach where the fickle weather obliged a second time. After, we went back to the Café Sympathique where I took part in, and enjoyed, the charming local custom of handshaking all round.

We went regularly to this same café for le petit déjeuner in the early mornings for the rest of our stay at this camp-site. The proprietors were gifted morale brokers.

There were unsettling moments at a different beach and at a bank. I had secured the vélo between two rocks at what I thought was a spot well above the high water mark. After a long walk along dunes and cliffs, I returned to leave for the day and stood in shock. The incoming sea had grabbed the vélo with all our attached precious belongings. The waves were thrashing angrily about the rocks where I thought I had left the bicycle — but there was something unfamiliar looking about the bay where I searched. The relief at finding the right bay and the vélo high, dry, safe and sound, was

30

inestimable.

The following day I read, and then fell asleep on the sand for several hours by a headland. Waking, I saw that the tide had cut us off from the other side of the point. There was nobody else in sight. Isolated, there was only one escape route and that was to go through the breakers holding the vélo overhead. The water was deeper than expected, and the struggle to get round the jutting granite was terrifying and painful as I wrestled to keep my transport out of the water, at least above saddle height.

After struggling for a quarter of an hour, I put the salt caked vélo triumphantly onto shingle and inspected the contents of the panniers. Mercifully all were fairly dry, protected by many plastic bags. Feet and legs, cut by rocks, were bleeding. I washed the grazes and superficial wounds in salt water while blood was gently oozing. After a little time platelets clotted, and the minor lacerations scabbed.

It was on a Monday that I first tried to change some money in Crozon, and I then learned that most banks in France do not open on that day, but do business normally on Saturdays. However I was able to find a 'credit' establishment that would do a transaction. Handing over fifty pounds sterling, I was asked for my passport. I unzipped the left hand inside pocket of the anorak and felt nothing. My stomach did the statutory somersault. Passport lost. And yet I could not believe it. I had, if anything, overfussed about this; routinely, sometimes unconsciously checking and rechecking the whereabouts and safety of valuables. I plunged again – deep into the pocket – and my arm kept going down. Shaking, I took the hand out and felt around the bottom hem on the outside of the garment – and there it was. The lining had burst and I would get this mended at a cordonnerie. Gleefully I signed the imperturbable cashier's paperwork, and even thought of offering him some of the francs which he handed over.

Next, on our slow way south, I found another gîte d'étape combined with a bar, restaurant and épicerie. Monsieur had a day job as a civil servant, and Madame and one of their daughters ran the establishment. I liked the ambience of this place, and after sampling the first dinner prepared by

31

Monsieur, did not want to leave. It was full of relish; he proudly said, when complimented that the cuisine was authentic Breton. Cooking was his hobby. He loved 'le plaisir de la table' and this presumably was his relaxation after difficult days working with the militaire – at what I was never clear. But he knew about Escoffier, and purred when I gave his establishment that name. Even better, we were in tranquil surroundings well off busy beaten tracks.

Trying to improve my French in the evenings, I would read the local paper over a few large glasses of expensive draught beer and tune in to the regulars' banter at the bar. The turnover was quick – it being generally unFrench or at any rate unBreton, to prop up bars for hours on end, and there was always mild surprise that I should want to succeed drink with drink quite so often and quickly. But after several days in what was to become known to me as The Crazy Dog Saloon, we better understood our cultural differences.

The family had three dogs. A German Shepherd, a German Shepherd cross, and a black and white type of English Setter or Spaniel. They were all amiably boisterous and it was there and it was then, that I put away for all time the measure of uneasiness, which with others, I had felt about the German Shepherd aka Alsatian. Our wrestling matches were hard fought and sporting.

I was the only long stay occupant of the smaller dormitory upstairs. There were no bunks – only mattresses on the floor. An amenity of this gîte was a large kitchen with table, utensils, fridge and a cooker powered by gaz, WCs, and showers with obnoxious, hair-plugged drains – and all within inconvenient olfactory distance: but I liked it here, and was in no rush to move on. A few people, including motorists, came and went, and on one occasion a young Australian couple stopped off with their vélos en route to St Malo and the ferry back to England. They were riding under time pressure as their visas would expire the following week. They were called Simon and Rachel and in the morning Simon shouted urgently from one of the cubicles, "Raitch – I need some paper – fast."

She went to a bag, said, "OK Sime – coming up," and from twenty paces, lobbed a roll over the door.

I stayed here about two and a half weeks enjoying a lazy routine of rising late, having large bowls of steaming café au lait for petit déjeuner, packing a grapefruit for a midday pause during long walks or rides through quiet countryside, and then preparing for Monsieur's evening feasts.

Once, I was invited by a heavy drinker to visit his boat the next morning for pastis. His wife was a busy and successful hairdresser, but he had retired. His equally bibulous pal drew numerous diagrams and maps on beer mats to indicate the route. I arrived at eleven to find my host smitten by a horrible hangover and transparently regretting his invitation to me a few hours earlier. Of his toping friend there was no sign — puzzling, because during the drinking bout he was most concerned that I should find the way. Soon, pastis by Ricard restored the captain to good form and the look of horizons came into his well charted eyes; so much that I worried lest he decided to cast off and make for Les Iles — his annual destination as soon as Madame had closed her salon for the holidays. He spoke gravely of the dangers of the sea — the more so as a medical customer of the Restaurant Escoffier had drowned in a tragic accident that week while taking guests out on his boat in the difficult, sometimes dangerous waters off Cap de la Chèvre.

'La Chèvre', more happily, was to feature again that very night in the restaurant. It was happy hour when a local regular with a laughing face and humour to match came in. He sold fitted kitchens for a living and strong willed would be Madame who could resist his pitch. He came into the room, looked around, and surprisingly, left without speaking. Shortly he reappeared with his lady on one arm, and with the other he held a long rope lead. At the end of this was a large and well behaved goat who gracefully took up a haunched position between the dining-tables and the bar. The dogs left and held a strategic conference outside. They returned and sat in a semi-circle in front of the motionless, serene, Madame La Chèvre — paying silent homage to their guest. If there was alarm in the hearts of the Escoffiers, it did not show. The goat's escort got on with his pastis, and observed approvingly that the animals were very calm.

That night at dinner half a dozen noisy and outwardly

menacing youths came in. Immediately there was hand-shaking all round. In England the word 'yobbos' would have come to mind. Their arrival did not change or trouble the atmosphere at all and I attended, with gusto, to boiling hot escargots, while looking forward to the next delicious surprise. Suddenly, one of the youths appeared at my table. He offered his hand which I shook — for the second time — and in the politest terms he asked if he could borrow the Dijon mustard to spread on the ham sandwiches he and his friends had ordered at the bar. In due course he replaced the jar with many thanks — and another handshake. By now I had become fascinated by the frequency of handshaking, and four cheek kisses, in this part of the world, and decided that these civilised habits could do nothing but make life easier.

Later, perhaps to honour Madame La Chèvre and the dogs, we all joined together for digestifs and had a festive time. The Patrons wanted me to assess Drake's prowess at boules on the 'oh' at 'Plymuss'. I said that he had won six championships in a row — which helped him to take better aim when he bowled much larger boules at the Spanish Armada. This went down well, all saying that they had not heard such news before; and they would not let me buy another drink that evening — generous fees for a dubious history lesson.

The weather on the morning after was awful with high winds and driving rain. There was no one else in the dormitory of the gîte d'étape. Depressed and hung over, I prepared for the day in the sanitaire. Afterwards, while bending over the stove to get a kettle going for tea, I cricked my back and could not move, stuck at forty-five degrees. I switched off the burner, and half a foot at a time, reached a chair which I used as a zimmer frame but could not hold anything like a mug. Nor could I carry milk from the fridge. It had to be black tea by the stove. I then hobbled a few steps to the table and made the mistake of sitting down. As soon as I had done this, I knew that I was immobile and in acute pain. It was, as the French say, a 'kattastroff'.

For two hours I rolled cigarette after cigarette, keeping the trunk as still as possible. The least movement was agony. No one came to the gîte and I had no idea what to do — marooned in pain — and suffering. Banging and shouting seemed

34

improper, and would hurt, but something had to be done. Something was done, rapidly, when I dropped a freshly lit cigarette into a small bin full of litter at the side of the chair. There was instant smoke. I had to pour water at all costs. Without thinking, in terror of a major fire, I got up from the chair, heard, rather than felt, a racking click — and found that I could actually put one foot in front of the other again. Before there was any flame, I doused the small outbreak and flooded the floor. I mopped up badly and then made more tea, this time with milk. But the pain recurred. What miraculous chance did I have of reaching Santander?

After two days there was no improvement. Sympathetic Madame having said "mon pauvre David" several times, made an appointment for me to see Madame, the capable, mature, blonde physiotherapist who wrestled with me for an hour and returned discs and other parts to their proper places. She then lectured me, using the word 'progressivement' often. Her diagnosis was that I had not been ready for long distance rides after a daily regime of short journeys to and from work in Plymouth. She rationed me to thirty kilometres a day for a week and said that I could increase this distance, but 'progressivement'. Madame of the gîte told me as we went back in her car that Madame the physiotherapist gave me no chance of getting even half way to Santander. The treatment cost one hundred francs which I paid gratefully, took her advice seriously, and had no further back trouble. Soon I was able to resume walking.

On the day before I left the Crazy Dog Saloon, I met a gang of council workers cleaning up a beach in a high wind. They were working hard and at speed. The men gathered up the debris, placing it in piles along the sand. It was a Saturday afternoon and I thought that by their industry, they were on a job and finish contract. Not so, as I learned when having stacked up all the rubbish, they found that they were without the means to set fire to it. The man in charge borrowed my lighter for an hour, depriving me of a smoke for what by my standards, was a long abstinence. Every now and then he would send a semaphore signal urgently from afar holding the lighter aloft thus assuring me that the thirty year old Ronson Varaflame was safe.

35

Chapter Four

The weather was bad on the following day when we left the Crazy Dog Saloon and its delightful family. The next stop was Telgruc sur Mer — a fairly short ride away. The clouds broke up and there was sunshine when we arrived at a well run campsite owned and operated by parents of two young, grown up, children. Monsieur had grey hair cut in a severe military style and spoke near perfect English. I told him in my imperfect French that I would rather hear the war experiences in his language. He grudgingly agreed and gave both shoulders a classic shrug. He had had a good war and his pro-British sentiment was obvious. He was, as an old soldier, indifferent to my tentlessness. He took me to a pitch on one of the well cut grass terraces and I left the sleeping gear on the ground before riding off to the town's Place for happy hour. The main bar in the centre provided a wooden dais for outside use and I settled cheerfully — a large glass of draught beer to hand. A car drew up alongside. A retired sort of citizen got out, and took the table next to mine. A rear door of the vehicle then opened, and struggling out was his disabled lady — emerging backwards. It took her about two minutes to move from the car with the imperative aid of a stick, and then somehow, to get up on our platform. The waiter had already brought two glasses of beer to their table, one of which Monsieur had nearly finished by the time Madame arrived. She took one sip out of hers, and then passed it, nearly full to him, which he quickly emptied. She paid, not a word was spoken. He rejoined his car, while she, unassisted, made her slow and awkward way back to it.

Returning to the campsite, I saw that a camion selling

fried food was in place. In charge of this huge kitchen on wheels were a couple of convivial young men from the south of France. An impromptu party got underway chaired by Mon Général and we all had much drink before he declared hunger and directed Madame to prepare a midnight snack in their caravan. She asked what crêpe fillings we would like, and when all was ready the Général rose and said to me in English, "Come, my friend, we will now have a crap together."

In the morning I went for a coast walk along the cliffs. There was nobody about and the wind was blustery. Taking a short-cut by road, I was passed by a man carrying fishing rods and shrimping nets over his shoulder. He wore a heavy leather jacket which almost, but not completely, concealed bare buttocks. Later, when I returned from the walk along the côte de sentier I saw him at work in the rock pools minus the top garment.

We left for Ploumordien and thought it proper that a Plymodien should be in the town. A rather ordinary dinner in an unremarkable hotel was followed by good sleep and morning departure for Quimper. After riding a few kilometres I felt a wobble on the front wheel. The countryside was desolate and a bit hilly, when we were caught in a sudden, long lasting cloud burst. We sheltered in a thicket but soon everything was sopping wet. On we went through intermittent rain.

When we reached Quimper, I asked for directions to a cycle shop and was told that we had already passed one on the outskirts. Reluctant to double back, I came to one a few doors down the street – run by a free spirit who had recently finished a round the world peregrination on his vélo which he proudly showed me. It lay in pieces on the workshop floor. He realigned the wheel and we set off south again, not sorry to be leaving the beautiful but crowded town with its pottery and thirteenth century cathedral. Not for the first time, I had followed a wrong road sign and was riding on the hard shoulder of another auto route express. We were admonished by the usual camion concertos – played loudly on French horns; but we had to keep going until the next exit road. There was no turning back. Before that we came to a service station – rare in that area – and rested with a

Mars bar and lemonade. After a wash and brush up, I got on the vélo and set off, riding for a few metres on a flat rear wheel. The disinterested fellow in the garage shop fetched an aerosol canister which he referred to as a 'berm'. He spoke in English, I, in French.

"Un berm Monsieur?" I asked.

"Yes," he replied, "a berm."

I had it. "Ah," I said knowingly, "Une bombe," and we understood each other.

He applied its nozzle to the air piece on the wheel. There was a great hissing and spilling of whipped cream. It oozed out all over vélo and onto the ground. I recalled this stuff first coming on the market: a sealing substance by which a punctured motorist could at least drive to a place of repair. This bombe cost about four and a half pounds — good value if it would keep us inflated for the ten kilometres to Concarneau.

I reckoned that the nearest exit road was about three kilometres away, and prayed that the gendarmes would not see us until we got off this forbidden auto route express. The berm/bombe was holding us up well at the back. We were riding at our highest gear speed on the hard shoulder when the exit road came in sight. As we approached the escape route, the whipped cream's hole plugging properties expired. The tyre flatulently gave up all its air. There were seven kilometres between us and Concarneau. The walk took an hour and a half, and night had already fallen as we passed a closed Peugeot cycle shop on the main road into the town.

By now I was exhausted, wanting only to hole up somewhere for the night. On the left-hand side there was a hotel. It could have been run by the founder of Pessimists Anonymous. Monsieur wore glasses and a beard. His teeth were shy as he half grinned, half smirked when he looked at the flat, ghostly white tyre. He listened to my news and loved it. He was happy, leading me up two flights of stairs to a hideous room where nothing worked. The Fakir's bed was narrow, water in the lavabo, occasional.

After the most elemental wash and brush-up I sought somewhere to eat. This was more elusive than I expected —

the town was full, but eventually I found a hot, uncomfortable place specialising in fish and fed moderately well.

Monsieur le Maître d'hotel was lugubriously dynamic in the morning at petit déjeuner when I told him of a bad sleep on a bed of nails. After paying the bill, and on the dot of nine o'clock, I arrived at the cycle shop, where an efficient, mature, overalled man put on and took off his glasses repeatedly while he inspected the rear wheel trouble. I wandered around for an hour, cheerfully remounting vélo in a weighty downpour of rain. There was a large supermarket on the outskirts of town where we sheltered until the heavy fall had passed.

We were now bound for Lorient via Quimperlé but the clouds and the rain persisted. Frequently I looked for shelter on the way to Pont Aven where we stopped for lunch under the awning of a café surrounded by many GB number plates. As I was having fish soup, an English woman in a group came close, had a good long stare in my bowl and said, "That looks good — let's have some." Then three Polynesian looking girls strolled by. There was much galleric tribute here to Paul Gauguin, and as this delicious trio hip swayed out of sight, I saw his 'Three Tahitians'.

We left for Briec. On the way there I saw a barely readable gîte d'étape sign pointing to a small road which we followed. This took us to an untidy farmyard full of clinging mud, and a variety of rubbish. No one was there and no dogs barked. I tapped on the window of what I took to be the main farmhouse. From the side, a youngish, dark haired, earth soiled, beautiful woman appeared.

I asked her if I could stay in the gîte. She smiled. "Of course. With pleasure." Wiping her slender, muddied hands on a kerchief, she showed me to a depository for old beds and mattresses in a two-storey building at the back of the farmyard. It was all in a state of fetid decay but at least, I thought, there could be some wine assisted oblivion in it. She looked like Mireille Matthieu. She agreed that I could have dinner at about nine o'clock, and returned to her back breaking work in a small field partnered by an elderly woman — probably Maman.

We rode the four kilometres or so to Briec to buy supplies

for happy hour. After this, I passed out in the sleeping-bag on top of an immense, weary mattress, and woke at 10.30 pm. Presumably, this was too late for dinner, but at the house there was no sign of life. The ladies were still working by a good daylight in the field as I went to them. Looking at my watch, I apologised for oversleeping — which puzzled them. They had no idea of the hour — there were no timepieces anywhere on the premises. I was told to go round to the kitchen where a very young woman was washing nettles and potatoes. It was Sybilla — a plump, blonde German girl who had coveted and found the good life here in this part of France. We talked and peeled the potatoes together; soon my hostess arrived. She lit a twig and branch fire in the huge hearth and hung an enormous black pot on a giant hook above the flames. She then poured water, and gently handed in the nettles and potatoes. When she had done this, Monsieur arrived — a bristled, ruddy faced, proud paysan bearing two large jugs of cider.

It was midnight before we set to the organic, delicious soup, pâté, bread, cheeses and cake — all produced on the self-sufficient farm. Here were calm, honestly self-contained, contented humans. They had an electricity supply from their own generator but no tractors — horses. No cars — bicycles. No chemicals. These three were among the least aggressive people I had ever met. They were undemanding of themselves and others, just getting on with life as they had moulded it, free of any vestiges of smug superiority. Without radio, newspapers and TV, they prospered and flourished in their unawareness and ignorance which gave them bliss.

Tranquil, I slept well and after home-made bread and jam, and with some reluctance, left this French family Robinson and made, over hilly terrain, for Quimperlé. The contrast with the world I had just left was violent. Cars, lorries and caravans were furiously driven as we approached the suburbs via a large trading estate. The rain was heavy and constant. Waterlogged, I went into a gas showroom at the bottom of the town seeking directions to a gîte d'étape, which from experience so far, provided the best doss down for one in my circumstances. Madame was patient and solicitous. She showed me maps and drew diagrams to a place on the other

40

side of town through which we had ridden earlier.

We set off in the non-stop rain and kept on pedalling in the sodden gloom, knowing that it would be pointless to wait. After asking for instructions several times, and by now thoroughly soaked and shivering, we arrived at a building with a big square courtyard, to be told by the kitchen staff of a smart restaurant, that the premises had changed hands. There had been no gîte d'étape here for three years. Fearing pneumonia, I asked for coffee. Surely, they said, a beer would be better? Madame passed me a small bottle of Kronenbourg. They declined payment and wished me well as we turned tail and aquaplaned back to Quimperlé to try and find a night's dry rest.

Up and down hills we went until, in what I thought was a separate town, we came upon a hotel in a quiet square. Yes, said le patron, there was a room for me and a garage (his own) in the house across the road, for the vélo.

It was now about seven o'clock and the main problem was drying out. The tobacco was too wet to roll and light, the green Rizzlas, pulpy. A timely brainwave intervened. I switched on the shaving mirror light in the lavabo recess. There was great heat from the small neon strip. Here was my dryer. I put socks and tobacco pouch on top of the light, pleased with my ingenuity. I turned the pouch over every few minutes and looked forward to the next smoke. When the tobacco was dry enough, I rolled up and poured Pernod in a tooth glass. Sitting in a dry towel on a chair by the small table, I decided that the world was not so foul after all.

I extinguished the smouldering socks just in time. There was the most awful stench at the moment of ignition. I dropped the abominable, brown, scorched offenders in the wash basin and opened the taps full blast. I wrapped them in tissue for the wastepaper basket. After hand mangling the rest of the rain drenched clothes, I went sockless to the dining-room, and had excellent consommé and turbot for dinner.

In the morning, I made a check-in 'phone call home. All was well, and we set off on the gradually flattening coast road towards Lorient. As it came in sight, we turned off the main road intending to idle for a few minutes on a beach

41

bench. A GB number plate let out six of my fellow countrymen and women, one of whom beat me to the bench I had
in mind. They seemed interested in the vélo and me, but I
did not bite when one of them said in good northern tones,
"That must be Lorient. Aye, that must be Lorient." Leaving
them to it, we went on our way and without too much
danger or difficulty found the ferry dock linking Lorient
with the Île de Groix which I wanted to visit for a day or so.

The crossing took about forty-five minutes but the handy
gîte d'étape on the island was full of holidaying school-
children; so I arranged for a relatively sumptuous stay at a
hotel overlooking the harbour and sea at about twenty-five
pounds a day for dinner, bed and breakfast. Demi pension.
The food was fishy and good, but the weather for the two
days I was there was even more dull than it had been further
north on the mainland. In the morning, on an exploratory
ride, I sheltered under the door porch of a closed beach-
side café for an hour, while the rain fell and went on falling,
with a strong Atlantic wind blowing ever more water clouds
across the island.

Two German shepherds appeared escorting Madame, who
opened up the café. I went in, and lingered for several
sheltered hours over coffee, beer, maps and a rather ordinary
plate of ham and chips. The radio was on at high volume and
I listened to Pierre, based in Paris, hosting a magazine show
with many fun games. He was obviously popular with
listeners. He teased them during the telephone quizzes. I
envied him not at all – prisoner though I was in this empty
seaside restaurant, albeit with a kind and talkative patronne.
At last in the early afternoon, the clouds broke up, and
scudding, even allowed us to see a little blue sky. We left in
the high, drying wind to do a circuit of the Île de Groix.

In the hotel dining-room that night and too close, at a
nearby table, was a party of British yachting people whose
tortured French was even worse than mine, and whose
general attitude as visitors, could not have done the entente
cordiale much good. Wishing that we were dining in different
places, I stopped the silent judging and condemnation, and
concentrated on the good oysters put before me together
with the thin, brown, locally buttered bread, and the near

42

freezing Chablis.

After dinner, I decided to take the morning ferry back to Lorient and went on a cognac crawl around the harbourside cafés. This provoked a dolefully boozy stocktaking of the caper so far. I was fed up with it; and with a surfeit of solitude — although that was something which, at the outset, I had cherished most. After a final Remy Martin, I was determined to junk the project. The ferry to ferry plan was laughable. Folly. Preposterous. I felt angry and defeated. I had the next final Remy Martin and black coffee knowing that in the morning I would enquire, in Lorient, about train or bus transport and rush to the South of France and perhaps when time was up, return to the UK by air. There would be no ignomy. I had casually mentioned to a few people that I was thinking, only thinking, about a Roscoff to Santander ride.

The inconvenience and self-inflicted torture were all but over. I left the bar and saw, on the quay, a couple coming towards me talking loudly and swaying. They were, like me, much in liquor. When over a certain alcohol limit, we tune instinctively to matching wavelengths. We three were old friends within the minute and went to a discotheque a short stagger away. Madame and Monsieur were middle-aged lovers who knew everyone in the place. He was a born islander, she from Lorient, and they were visiting friends and relatives while he enjoyed leave from his job as a cook aboard an oil tanker plying in the Orient. Monsieur spent little time at our table, catching up, as he had to, with all his many friends. He put me in charge of Madame, who shouted at me every moment or so above the raucous music and told me of her great, endless love for Monsieur. It was a costly, drunken, time and I could not safely ride vélo the few hundred metres to the ferry in the morning.

The short sea voyage cleared the head a bit. We arrived back in Lorient and heard church bells. It was Sunday and travel agents and transport offices would be closed. Should we stay until the next day or pedal on? I knew that by riding, the terrible hangover would get no worse, but there was serious fatigue in the leg motors. We turned right, continuing the foolishness. By keeping the sea to hand and getting lost only twice, we were able to clear Lorient and pulled up at a well run chambre d'hôte near Plage Monteno. At this stage I was in a state of mental limbo, devoid of all resolve and plans and so far as I could decide anything, left the future to winds and fate. Sleep here was sound, and after petit déjeuner, tidily served by Madame (and with toast for the first time − instead of bread and croissant) we left for Plage Monteno where there was a campsite with mobile homes for rent. Although expensive, and bookable only by the week, I decided to anchor there. I would consolidate and think out the next moves; sleep regularly and fairly comfortably; use the laverie to clean up the dirty clothing − an ever present, bothersome worry.

The rooted caravan was entirely self-contained, but although instructed in its use, I funked the gas hot water boiler, using everything else however, including the cooker for soup, ravioli and other tinned fare obtainable from the owner's shop. There was one major problem. Campsites in France do not accept payment by plastic. They will honour Euro or travellers' cheques, but I had neither. The proprietors allowed me to stay the first night − trusting me to get cash from a bank in nearby Plouhinec the next morning, and recommended the Crédit Agricole branch.

The night was hot, and hungry mosquitoes dive-bombed like Stukas leaving bloody trophy marks on the bed clothes generously lent by Madame.

We rode the seven or eight kilometres to Plouhinec to be told by all five banks in the town that they were too small for plastic transactions − in my case Access and Visa. The bankers suggested Port Louis but I was aware that closing time was near and having promised that I would settle with cash that day to pay a week's rental in advance, I was now seriously worried that the campsite owners would regard me as a con man and bounce us out.

I calculated time and distance, and set off at top speed on mercifully flat roads for Port Louis. En route we passed through Riantec and saw another, much bigger, branch of Crédit Agricole. To stop or not to stop was now the question. I did not want to lose time in enquiry and arrive too late in Port Louis. However, I gambled − and won. A tall, studious

44

man behind the counter said "Oui" and pointed to the outside, explaining that there was 'a hole in the wall' cash dispensing machine by the door; but I did not know how to work it — never having tried one in the UK. By now I was in a state of optimistic excitement, sure that I could return honourably to Plage Monteno. I gabbled at the man in poor French, who blinked, and kept on blinking, not understanding a word of my outpouring. He suggested that we try speaking in English. I drew breath, calmed down, and we carried on in French. He lead me to the machine and quietly asked for the amount. I whispered it. Eighteen hundred francs please. When he told me to press the PIN number, he coyly looked away and then resumed his button pushing. There was a long, long, wait while the gizmo spoke to London relatives in a question and answer session. All was quiet. Suddenly there was a gurgling sound from the orifice, and a smile on bank man's face. Like a midwife delivering a baby, he gently lifted the money with both hands, checked it all over, and carefully passed the precious bundle to me. I spoke to him as a rescued sailor would speak to the crew of a lifeboat; and then spent an hour longer than necessary on the return journey by taking too many wrong turnings. I paid my dues, and features relaxed all round.

In this area, there were beaches as far as the eye could see. One day in pleasingly warm weather I walked for miles in the general direction of Lorient, passing a block house here and there — leftovers from German occupation. A few people were sunbathing and windsurfing on the other side of one of these structures. Some ladies were topless but none bottomless as well, save one. She, wearing a one piece silvery bathing costume, when I first saw her, had just come out of the sea and was returning to her pitch upon the sand by the dune.

She took off the swimwear, showing a lithe, beautifully tuned and toned, copper coloured body. She moved and walked like a ballet dancer. Quite unselfconsciously she stretched out on her green patterned towel — uniquely naked on the beach — and tried to light a cigarette. She was having trouble with her briquet. I lent her mine. I complimented her on such a graceful walk over the hard sandy

45

going on the beach and asked if she was a dancer. She smiled, said yes, thanked me for the light, and explained that she was a member of a Paris based corps of Baroque ballet. Passers-by took not the slightest notice as she sunbathed, smoked and read. Libre.

Chapter Five

The week passed after a restful time spent mainly walking and riding around the area, sun and sea bathing. On the way to this Plouhinec district I had bypassed Port Louis so decided to double back a bit and have a look at it. This was a wise move — if only for the dinner that night at a two star hotel where I had checked in for the one night. There was no bar, but aperitifs were being served in the reception area when I came down. Several couples, senior in appearance, looked hungrily at their watches as seven o'clock approached. On the dot, the area emptied and we all made for the dining-room where there was good space between the tables. Monsieur le Chef, who was also the Patron, had been pacing up and down. He now went to his kitchen. Dinner was a five course affair, perfect in quality, presentation and service. There was near silence. Conversation was confined to quiet, respectful, murmurs — akin to softly said prayers of thanksgiving in church; broken, now and again, only by the muffled, reverential report of a well modulated belch.

The feast took nearly two hours and the experience was so overwhelming that I forgot to note the gastronomic items and cannot now remember a single dish. I recall only questions about this meal. Was its creator a scion or protégé of Anatole? Had we been fed by one holding the secrets of Mrs Travers' kitchen at Brinkley Court? Would Bertie Wooster have drooled here as he did in Worcs? I guessed that P.G. Wodehouse had eaten here; and Aunt Dahlia herself would have pouted with pleasure. It was so moving that I booked in for a second night to dine again at this place with its resident genius.

47

After a good sleep, and early morning anticipation of seven pm, I walked around, filling in time, and had a haircut by an attractive young woman running her own salon. She did a tidy and thorough job but took too literally my request that it should be short. The lady left me only millimetres away from a brush cut. Then to a pissoir in the town square. I pressed the button to flush out the urinal and was firmly pushed back a few feet by a jet as strong as a small water cannon. Luckily the day was fine, and the air hot, so that in about fifteen minutes the clothes were dry again after a walk down to the harbour to take a boat across the estuary to Lorient. On the way I saw, and paused at, a brand new Tuna fishing vessel. It was commanded by a skipper from St. Pierre and Miquelon — French territories off the east coast of Canada. He invited me aboard and we chatted easily. He showed me around his up-to-date, but cramped, vessel, designed to fish in the Mediterranean. The ship carried a crew of seven and they were off that afternoon to the Île de Groix for sea and equipment trials. This diversion and the crossing to Lorient were merely time wasters until seven o'clock when the dining-room would be ready again.

Time dragged; and I had not anticipated Anatole's volatility. The atmosphere, at aperitif time, was uneasily tense. Anatole paced faster and faster. There was fury in his step. He daggered Madame with his eyes and burnt her with his beard. Something terrible had happened. Madame, working at her desk, did not hear my greeting or my suggestion that their dining-room should be called the 'Bon Appetit'.

The guests' faces, though still slightly expectant, wore disappointed, sombre expressions. I had formed the impression that an annual visit here had become the high spot of their retired lives; and as with those who expect some rain to fall every year at Bognor, so were my fellow guests philosophical and resigned this night. Anatole and his lady had declared war (again) and the fallout was everywhere. The staff were obviously troubled. I recall the unopened oysters. I could not prise them successfully, and although my surgical bungling could be both seen and heard in the silent, unhappy room, no help was offered — neither did I ask for it. I remember those oysters for the wrong reasons, and was

48

miserably disappointed that my extra night had coincided with a round of regular in-house hostilities.

In the morning I fastened the panniers on the vélo which had been parked alongside a tree in the garden. Fortunately there had been no rain to make the handlebar chrome even rustier. After petit déjeuner during which I tactfully avoided communion with Anatole and Madame, we set off for the Golf de Morbihan. The riding was pleasant and before we reached Le Bono – our next stop, we were passed by a car which slowed and then parked on the grass verge. It was driven by an American woman on her own who needed map help. She was a teacher from Michigan and was flustered – she wanted to reach Carnac, and time was short for her return to St. Malo and the ferry back to Portsmouth. According to my map reading she was on the right road, and I wished her well as we both resumed our journeys.

The descent to Le Bono was steep. Of much local interest was the old wooden bridge. It looked, to me, like any other old wooden bridge. I did not, and made no effort to, understand what the fuss was all about. There was a room at one of the two or three small hotels in the sleepy waterside village. My host was annoyingly indifferent to my story as I checked into a somewhat primitive room with peeling wallpaper and uncertain lavabo.

We rode down to a small dock where an excursion vessel was about to leave on a four hour journey to the Gulf waters and Islands. I chatted with a couple of ladies who were selling tickets for the trip but decided not to go. They were comfortingly interested in my news, and put questions. Santander – in Spain? They looked at me and at the vélo and laughing, kindly shook their heads: but their interest inspired me.

"Perhaps you will read the book?"

"You are a writer?"

I smiled a silly smile. "Possibly," I replied, and smirked when they said that I could count on them to read it – even though they expected the story to end long before Spain, let alone Santander.

The weather was perfect as I walked to the tidal inlet at Bono where every prospect pleased, and only the beach was vile – consisting of revolting muddy slime; but I found a dry

49

gravelly patch where two mothers and their children were playing. We chatted and I said that there were few, if any, tourists here even though it was high season.

"Where you have beautiful sand," one of them said, "you have the world. We prefer mud and no people."

After dinner (steak and chips) I met some convivial local people. We drank far into the night and the morning hangover, painful as usual, was bested as usual, by a good run on the vélo — as effective a cure as any I had ever found. En route to Vannes we burnt up the kilometres, and by the time we got there at noonish I had fully recovered, was in a lather, and gasping for cold beer which I found at a pleasant place on the river front. It was owned by a congenial middle-aged cycling enthusiast who calculated distance run from Roscoff and kilometres to Santander. He estimated about nine hundred. Tired, I decided to stay the night in Vannes, described by Monsieur as 'bourgeois'. Unfortunately there were no rooms at this pleasant man's establishment, and we had to ride long and hard out of Vannes before reversing and finding a Holiday Inn sort of lodging near the centre.

The town was packed with people, cars and coaches, one of which was parked outside the hotel, carrying English tourists from the north. On my way to the en suite room I was lucky enough to get, I held the door of the lift open for one of them. "Mersey," he said politely, and I returned his goodwill.

This hotel would give me the opportunity to have a bath for the first time since leaving Plymouth and I looked forward to a good, long wallow. The room was priced at about twenty-eight pounds — expensive by previous French standards but cheap by comparison with UK (especially London) prices. The coach party members had a separate dining-room. In the place where I sat down, several people were feeding alone and there was no sound save that of bottle, glass, cutlery and plate. We were all preoccupied with ourselves; and I conjectured that the others were all staying in this commercial hotel because they were in Vannes on business. For table company they had books, newspapers, or magazines, while I found companionship in the diary and ball-point pen. With café cognac I rolled a cigarette, and noticed that the filling cap cover on the lighter was missing. I had a good look around on and under the table and was surprised that at petit déjeuner the next morning, the waitress, who had searched with me the night before, asked if I had found it. I had not, told her that I appreciated her concern, and said that the loss was not serious.

The vélo had spent the night in the electronically secure underground garage and I was given a special entry code to it when checking out. Expecting difficulty, having already forgotten the instructions and not being brave enough to return for a refresher course, I was saved by a brief-case carrying motorist who, by making the right contacts, got the heavy doors obeying at once. Afraid of finding ourselves again on forbidden auto route expressways, it took us two hours to get out of Vannes bound for the next staging point — Allaire.

At last we found the right road after many mistakes and enquiries; but I soon began to feel woozy with occasional panic spasms. When this came on, I stopped at the roadside, and put the passing indisposition down to fear, dehydration, and over exertion, but not, this day, to a hangover. The spirit level plunged, but I perked up easily and quickly, at an isolated restaurant for camionneurs — the best type of transport café endorsed and recommended by Les Routiers. After moderate hydration, I went into the dining-room where no-nonsense Madame briskly took me to a table for four already occupied by three others. The room and lorry park were full, and mine was the only empty chair.

My fellow users welcomed me warmly, realising that I did not know the form. Peckish, I took three slices of charcuterie brawn when the ration was two. Madame spotted this and ticked me off. I offered to return the excess piece to the communal plate, but my table mates laughed, and would have none of it. Soon there arrived the most delicious food with good wine, the camionneurs drinking little; and there was cheerful, jokey talk. There were four removes altogether, with a choice for the main dish between fish and lamb stew which could have been prepared, on a peace day, by Anatole himself. The bill, in all, was forty-seven francs — under five pounds.

We continued in high humidity to Allaire, stopping at a front-room-come-bar run by an outstandingly fat man who had once been to sea, and who gave the impression that he would like to be there still. Conversation with him was hard pounding, and I wondered why he bothered to let the world in through his open door.

The air was close, clammy, and unpleasant to breathe when we got to Allaire. There, I booked into a room a few feet away from a clock tower that chimed ear-splittingly every fifteen minutes. We were invited to park the bicycle at the establishment's open urinal in the backyard. The arrangement unsettled me, but Madame was confident that vélo would be safe and dry. For this I offered silent thanks in advance for the dignified safe-keeping of the blessed machine, my indispensable ally.

It was hot and stuffy in the restaurant which I chose for dinner. There was a general air of unhappiness, maybe due to the suffocatingly oppressive weather. There was little charm or cheerfulness that I could sense, and only two or three eating places for choice. I was sweatingly uncomfortable in the one I selected; and I was encircled by similarly bothered families from Scotland and London. I concentrated on the diary notes — looking forward to paying the bill and having cognac elsewhere. Sleeping badly, bonged every quarter hour by fairly Big Ben outside the window, I tried to bathe in the deep well of a tub in the early morning. As I went to it, I stepped on a non-ledge, and came close to orthopaedic treatment. I was saved by a soap dish on the wall to which I clung, preventing a bone fracturing fall.

Vélo, I was relieved to observe, had not been wetted upon from a great height, and we set off on a road that would take us north of Nantes. I decided to cross the Loire at Ancenis, keeping with our practice of avoiding big busy places where and when that could be done. The countryside was noticeably flatter now, and we made pleasingly fast times when actually in the saddle. The dérailleurs were thlunking away melodiously. Soon we were in a densely forested area, and at about noon I spotted a sign to an auberge with horsemen and women riding by. This was an elegant building — at first sight a mini château — and I was effusively welcomed by the aubergiste wearing a snow-white apron around a well fed waist. Surprised at my fears, he nevertheless seated me at a window table from where I could look out on my vélo, and the cavaliers on their horses.

A dozen jolly horsey folk shared a table, and were in high spirits. They were obviously having a good day in their saddles. Their mounts were also lunching well as they grazed peacefully on luscious grass around the inn. Even though late, I was brought tasty and satisfying food: poached salmon, steak and cheeses — sent down by a well chilled bottle of Muscadet. We then left and made more quick headway through the heavily forested terrain. Such was the ordered configuration of the trees that I presumed they had been planted and lined up by the local equivalent of the forestry commission. When it was late afternoon, I thought it time to think about a sleeping place for the night.

In the flat, windless conditions, we made good and easy time in our highest effortless gear to another signposted auberge in the forest. The road was all but deserted. We turned left and after thirty more minutes of delightful riding came to a crossroads in the woods. In one corner of this carrefour there was a huge pile of logs. On top sat a man holding a large wooden home-made cosh. It was fastened to a piece of rope anchored to his belt.

We stopped and I asked him how far we were from the auberge.

"About five kilometres," he said.

A car was parked nearby. The thin sound of a female wail came from the forest. Quizzically, and a touch alarmed, I looked about me. There was something spooky in the atmosphere.

"That is my wife," the man said. "We come here so that she can disappear in the forest and this noise is her signal to me that all is well. There are many funny people hereabouts."

When I apologised for my poor French (explaining, as I did every time, that I had to think in English and then translate the thoughts) he said in good English, "That's all right — you speak French just like Laurel and Hardy."

His lady duly appeared, but not before a few more agreed

wails, and they took out photographs from the car boot. He had been a pilot with Air France and from the pictures, I could see that they lived in an idyllic mill stream house some fifty kilometres away.

We went on riding, not without a few eerie feelings. We were the only people about. Vélo had long ago become a people. More, many more than five kilometres on (surely the pilot would have estimated distances better when flying) we arrived in heavy, cloying overcast at the inn, run alone by Madame whose only and much loved son was doing army service, for the compulsory year, in Grenoble. Dinner and sleep were good — the latter in a relatively comfortable bed.

After petit déjeuner in the morning I tried several times to call home for check-up purposes. This was from the coin box in the hall of the auberge. After half a dozen attempts there was no reply and I became anxious. My wife, who comes and goes a great deal on her various activities, could, though, be almost guaranteed to answer the 'phone at 8 am. Finally we made contact. All was well, but the bell on the downstairs handset had failed. I asked her to get it mended as quickly as possible: I did not want to sweat like that again — even for a few minutes. This she did by the time I called again a couple of days later.

These check-in calls were vitally important — and not just for the obvious reasons of passing messages, if any. With so much time alone on the saddle of a bicycle bad thoughts, if not controlled, can easily invade one's mind. It was only after we got back, that our son told me of an attempted midnight break-in around mid-July. Someone had broken the glass on top of the front door but ran off after lacerating himself — leaving a trail of fast flowing blood. One of the two policemen who arrived rapidly on the scene said, "Let's hope he bleeds to death." But I was told nothing about this terrifying incident when I made check-in calls after it. Had I known, morbid fear might have been impossible to repulse, and our mission, probably aborted.

We left the forest and set course for Ancenis — which would take us north of, and away from, Nantes. This is where at midday the rain began and poured heavily for hours. I put the vélo under verandah cover, and lunched stickily in a packed restaurant patronised on that day by large numbers of my fellow countrymen and women. The room was adhesively hot — the service irritatingly slow, and when food came, I ate in misery. The rain lashed and lashed and I thought again about trains and coaches and lifts with lorries and a quick return to Roscoff and the ferry back to Plymouth. It all seemed then, in that steaming eating place, so pointless, so idiotic. When people asked me why I was going to do this, the bad best I could offer was "Because the roads are there." This satisfied no one. Then I would say "God only knows the reason for it, and He doesn't tell me. Definitely, I am not required to know." There the matter always rests. It is not a keep-fit exercise, nor a sight-seeing tour. Whatever the motivation; book material, greater knowledge of cycling, of France and of Spain, could all be put aside as honest reasons. I did not know then, do not know now, and expect never to know the answer to the depressing, futile, question, "Why are you doing this?" Who, in any case, really cares? Those rancid considerations apart, the ecstasy of going with the wind when it and one's own mood match is a good enough taste of heaven. Sweating and downcast, I did not wait for coffee and went to the bar for a digestif.

Here my spirits rose — there was repair for the broken soul. It came from the laughter of a man whose mirthful consumption of life is such that his sound should be amplified around the world wherever there is anguish in human hearts. It was lucky, lovely, loveable laughter. It was like the hee-haw of a donkey in delirium who has just been told that it is not to be Blackpool Sands this year — but a mixed sanctuary in Sidmouth instead.

There was more to come as my second cognac arrived. A large, merry, and well lunched gentleman invited me to meet his wife at home. He had been in the French Commando. His last posting had been in Africa for two years and he had retired in the rank of Colonel. With the African garrison behind him, he was now keenly getting down to a good helping of overdue hedonism. His invitation, confirmed after he had telephoned Madame, was for drink, music, and dance. His transport was 'Un camping car' — a small motor caravan.

55

I was afraid as we set off — he was quite drunk — and I thought, as we slowly wove along, of my own transgression ten years before. Although he gripped the wheel authoritatively, his control was quite impaired and soon we bounced off a hedge on my side of the vehicle. Not a seat belt was in sight, but this hit 'sobered' him enough to continue without further trouble.

His lady greeted him fulsomely, and he started to play the piano. I could not recognise any of the tunes, but kept him going with 'Bravo', after 'Bravo'.

"Maestro," I said once. This pleased him and he banged the keys with even more brio.

"Merde," said Madame, who during the fortissimo passages told me what a ghastly life she led married to this drunken hulk, whose capacity for liquor surpassed that of Bacchus himself.

Cassettes of Irish folk songs were played. Madame cried, and told me that she was not moved by the music, but that it was convenient cover for her to blub — as she did every day over what she described as her 'miserable life'. Then, out of remorse perhaps, she would embrace her man, sometimes in a painfully embarrassing, unselfconscious way. They danced in eyebrow raising intimacy. When the music stopped, Monsieur produced a formidable assortment of firewater bottles all of which he insisted, ordered, must be tried. Some of this drink was so potent and fabric altering, that it stained teeth as I saw later. Much later.

Although happy and suitably en rapport with my hosts, I was fretting about the safety of the vélo which I had left outside the restaurant. The former warrior took my anguish almost as an affront — a near insult to France. He assured me again and again that people do not steal bicycles in France.

"But don't they steal money, passports, tickets and credit cards?" I asked — for all these things were on the vélo.

"Non, non, non," he roared, and foamed slightly at the mouth. "THIS IS FRANCE." He lectured me about the greatness of his country, its gloire and the honesty of its people. Only when he offered to collect it in the camping car did I stop worrying and got on with the party. De Gaulle would have been proud of him.

At three in the morning Madame produced moules marinièrs and Coquille St. Jacques. It was highly delightful blotting paper. I asked where the moules in Brittany came from. My host appeared to be something of an expert on the subject, and said that the best places were St. Brieuc and Quimperlé. He gave a long explanation on the quality of the coastal waters switching now and then to English which I could not always follow. When he referred to "much peeg sheet in zee vassair" I tried to think of white wine sauce instead. As I voraciously scooped mollusc flesh from the shells I was not curious to know whether the moules were attracted to, or repelled by, this material in the sea around the shore. At four am I was invited to play the piano and obliged with the bass part of chopsticks — asking first if it should be in waltz, fox-trot, or quickstep tempo. They did not know this piece — the only item in my own repertoire — and left the choice to me. I played the monotonous chords at all three speeds without treble accompaniment. Even though one of the keys I required was mute, the performance moved my new friends: he showed his feelings with prolonged o-la las, she with sniffles and sobs.

Although I cannot remember going to a bed, I woke up in one. Sunlight was dazzling my sore eyes and the music of Monsieur on the piano was hurting my ears. My teeth had gone soft and my hair was painful. I went through searing spasms of worry and remorse. I had no toothbrush to remove the incendiary stains from my charcoal grey teeth, and felt helpless all over.

Luckily the old warrior drove us safely back to the vélo to which he pointed smugly. All was well. The vélo was secure and I tried to convince my host that I had not really been worried. After cleaning up as best I could in the restaurant's WC, we set off for Ancenis in the heart of Gros Plant Muscadet country before heading for the coast again, and the navigational aid of the sea on our right as we pedalled on southward. Some lively riding helped to expel and sweat out most of the crudy hangover vapours. When we arrived in the late afternoon, Ancenis seemed to have closed down — with the exception of a room only hotel, and a salad café in the Place.

57

Chapter Six

In the morning we rode over the bridge, glancing at the low, ebbed, muddy water below. Here was a milestone for us. Patting a handlebar, I praised vélo and said aloud, "The Loire is behind us." As we went along part of the famous valley, we saw many buses with dozens of bicycles on their roofs. Having seen Loire Valley Cycling Holiday advertisements, I knew that baggage was transported ahead, but thought that their bicycles were for riding. Complacently, I invited the vélo to get an eyeful.

The next stop was Clisson and we bucked a strong headwind all the way. At a roundabout and going in the opposite direction, we saw a couple aboard a heavy laden tandem. We waved greetings, as cyclists do in France, and an hour later, stopped at a lay-by caravan refreshment stall. Soon after, the tandem arrived and we talked. They had cleverly dealt with the rain by fashioning head holes in light blue plastic bin liners and were as bone dry as if they had dressed in sou'westers. He was bearded, English and a serious cyclist. She, darkly beautiful, athletic, French and a maths teacher from Quimperlé. He had been based in Cornwall but came from the Midlands. Divorced with three children, the tandem commander was now very happy living and riding with the maths teacher in France. They were a pleasant couple, also on a long journey. The two were bound for Aix-en-Provence and were under deadline pressure. They intended to do a thousand miles in fewer than ten days. To them an average of one hundred and forty kilometres a day was a normal accomplishment, whereas if we had put eighty kilometres on the clock after a day's ride, we had won the Tour de France.

When I told them about my Roscoff-Santander objective, he spoke genuinely encouraging words. "You'll do it." No one had said that before, and I was elated. Then we got on our bikes, and went our separate ways.

The weather in Clisson was dismal. It too was a place with an inexplicable commercial ghostliness. I was able to get a room in a centrally located hotel, but could find only a greasy spoon café for dinner. The place was full of flies and noise, as youngsters played maniacally with the games machines. In spite of the tandem riders brief pep talk I was down again, and tried hard to avoid thinking about the kitchen in these premises.

The dining area was empty when I arrived, but shortly after, a middle-aged English couple came in and took the table next to mine. They spoke loudly in English and I winced at the obvious, quick, dislike between them and the waiter. When the woman was asked if she would like cheeses she said, "Frommidge? All right then, I'll have a bit of cheese."

I walked back to the hotel determined this time to truncate the mad, ridiculous journey. Usually, every night, I checked the vélo's tyre pressures wherever it was housed — mostly in sheds and garages. This time I did not bother; and even hoped that it might be stolen before morning. If it was still there I would put it on a train, and we would go to the South of France, and, when time was up, fly back to the UK as I had planned in Lorient on that Sunday when everything was closed.

The train station was sepulchral, and the hour late, and I went in to start the business of arranging our transport to Marseilles. I had already in my hand the magic plastic money card, but the clerk took no notice. He became deeply interested, however, when I mentioned the vélo, and, animated, he told me enthusiastically that there were so few trains in France which carried bicycles that I might as well abandon the idea for ever. Theoretically, it would have been possible for us both to have reached Marseilles by train, but the hassle and aggravation would have been enormous. I was surprised to learn that in vélo loving France, La Petite Reine and train do not go together much. Perhaps this is a policy to encourage maximum use of the most efficient item of engineering ever invented.

I took this as a sign. There must be no more belly-aching. No more furious defeatism. We must carry on and not cheat by train, coach, car or lorry. We must keep right on to the end of the road in Santander. We must ride (or walk) every centimetre of the way. I went to the vélo, checked everything, and gave it the latest news. This done, I had a fortifying café cognac or three, and in the hotel bar softly sang *Daisybell* and *Les bicyclettes de Belsize*.

By this time all my clothing was putrid and offensive to me. In Challans, en route to the coast again, I hoped to find a hotel with some sort of bath so that I could do something to freshen up, if not wash clean, my reeking things.

I checked in at yet another room only hotel and was shown to en suite quarters with basin, bidet, and shower but no tub. There was garage space for the vélo, and for the first time I removed all four panniers, back and front, and carried them and their ponging contents upstairs. Then, wearing one of the house towels only and steaming like a kettle on the boil (the air temperature was in the nineties) I took more than an hour to soap and rinse everything I had with me. In the bathroom there was a brand new lavatory brush still in its wrapper, and with this I scrubbed (in the bidet) the black trainers, the once white tennis shoes, the replacement flipflops. Exhausted, I recuperated with tobacco and cognac. Then I put on soaking wet shirt, drawers, and trousers, felt much better, and went out looking for somewhere to eat. As with so many hotels I had come across recently, this one provided no food — with the exception of breakfast coffee, bread and croissants.

Handily there was a crêperie, and it was while I sat at table with wine and pancakes, writing up the day's notes, that a woman and her daughter came in. Something was seriously wrong. The young woman lay down on the floor face up. Her pallor was disturbing — almost translucent. For a moment I thought she had died. The words of Bach's St. Matthew Passion came to me. 'Death's pallid hue comes o'er thee — the glow of life decays.' I judged her to be about twenty, with Titian hair and angelic features. She was a frightening sight. It turned out that we three were staying at the same hotel, but daughter was all in, and could not walk the short distance back. A doctor was called, arrived, and diagnosed serious sunstroke.

I slept well in the hot night and had petit déjeuner in a small upstairs room. Madame was in good form, and with increasing facility I spun her my yarn and plans. Asking forgiveness for my poor French (the grovel always worked) elicited loud disagreement. My hostess asked if I were an English professor teaching French in England? I thought it not proper to ask if she were a French professor teaching psychology in Challans? She had beguiled me, and I was set up for the day. There was more to come. A bubbly and lovely flaxen haired girl at a bank, who helped me with the cash machine, also praised my French. How right these ladies of Challans were. And how wrong was the cosh carrier in the forest. Laurel and Hardy, forsooth.

The distance to Saint Jean de Monts on the coast was about fifteen kilometres, but losing the way, we stopped at a carrefour to do some map reading. A car slowed down and the couple in it offered to help, and gave me good, clear directions. They were amicable. We talked briefly, and they said that there were many British tourists in the vicinity, and especially on the coast. This I already knew — the roads were full of GB plates. They drove off, and I took the same road. We were very much in holiday home country and a few kilometres on I was taken by the bijou look of a magnified doll's house — predominantly white, picked out in shining astral blue. As we approached, a man and a woman waved us down. They were our helpers in the car at the crossroads. It was the hour of déjeuner.

"Come for a drink," they said, "and if you have time, some lunch as well."

We parked under the shade-giving tree, and spent a couple of cordial hours with them and their son who was learning to become a musician. They were based in Paris. He, a dentist; she, a functionary with a Government third world aid department. This was good, warm, hospitality — even better for it being such a pleasant surprise. After some cold beer, we had lettuce salad with vinaigrette and lamb chops grilled over garden wood in the disproportionately large fireplace. Son suggested the outside barbecue, but he was overruled by Maman who said that it was too hot. I was glad that vélo was resting in cool shade, as I had, on leaving Challans, given both tyres good, long, pumpings.

Jacques, whose face was open full, and Marie France — dark haired, attractive, preserved and poised, were as charming a couple as any lost itinerant cyclist could ever hope to meet; and they were truly interested in my doings. Red wine flowed with the tenderly done chops. Marie France, talking well, at one point upset her full glass onto the waiting cheeseboard. Pausing only for the obligatory 'merde', she did not break the flow of her theme, floating balletically from table to cupboard and mopping cloth. I was in good heart, and hoped that fate would allow us to meet another day.

Vélo and I began again buoyantly, well stimulated by this perfect knight of the road and his lady. At about five o'clock we arrived at a campsite on the coast south of Saint Jean de Monts. I asked middle-aged Madame at reception if I could rent a tent or caravan for a few days, as I wanted now to let a bit of grass grow under us. Lately there had been too many rushed one night stays, and I was weary of handling things in and out of the panniers so frequently, and having to guess chaotically where wanted pieces were, after haphazard packing. At this stage I was craving the ordinary conveniences of home — running hot and cold water, shelves holding toothpaste, brush, soap dish, teapot, clean towels, slippers, ice to go with whisky. Hooks to hang things on.

Madame pointed to a caravan with a living-room tent attached. "Thank you," I said happily. "That will do very well, Madame." As she reached for the key on a board behind her desk, there was an earsplitting, nerve shattering explosion. It was either gun fire, or a bomb. Frozen with fright, we looked at each other thinking of only one thing, asking but one question. Did the detonation come from a time set bomb, or was the gunman outside? Campers all over the large site erupted.

"Terroristes, terroristes, terroristes," they screamed, "Bombe, bombe, bombe."

We, alone together in the office, stayed put and waited,

glancing furtively out of the window, crouching low. Five minutes passed, and nothing else happened. The holiday-makers spoke more calmly. There were no more reports. Madame and I agreed that it was a frightening mystery. Soon the campers returned to their ping-pong, sunbathing, barbecues, children's swings and tiny roundabouts.

We sounded the all clear and set off for the caravan some fifty metres away, collecting the vélo en route and wheeling it in step with my hostess. Something was amiss. The rear wheel was flat. A large amount of inner-tube fouled the spokes and there was a great rent in the tyre itself. It had burst – this had been our bomb. The blow-out was presumably caused by heat and hyper-inflation. It was our explosion that had nearly arrested hundreds of holidaying hearts. The word soon spread, and we became instant celebrities. The place was teeming with teenagers who thought the whole business a mega hoot. They referred to me thereafter as Monsieur Bombe.

For us this was a catastrophe. Un gron katastroff. But the contents of the caravan cheered me up a bit. No running water, but a fridge, gaz cooker, table and chairs. Madame of the fuller, more comfortable figure, blonde and bespectacled, told me to take everything off the vélo and to leave the whole lot inside the tent while we all went by car to St. Hilaire some seven kilometres away to find a bicycle repair man – if it was not too late. I had forgotten that in France most premises stay open until at least seven pm. It was nearly six o'clock when we left in her small hatchback. The vélo was reluctant to join us, and I had to wrestle it into the rear end of the car with the front hanging and banging around outside.

The first expert was 'complet' but could do the job next morning. I did not want to part with vélo overnight – there would be the worry of arranging transport from the campsite, and busy Madame had already done enough. She was a brick, and we tried another place. The Gauloise smoking mechanic, surrounded by several vélos, all in pieces, nodded wearily and ordered me to return in half an hour. Madame left for the campsite saying that she hoped I would get back safely. I thanked her ardently for such goodness to me in this crisis, and drank the lady's health in cold beer at a nearby bar, and thought happily about, and saluted, the good, generous, 'can do' people I had met that day.

The vélo with a brand new tyre and inner-tube on the rear wheel was ready on time and cost about twelve pounds. I found my way back to 'Le Camping' (Kommping) quite easily to be greeted excitedly by the adolescent brigade. Evidently I had become a hero figure after the explosion — for frightening the life out of their parents. My quarters were of immense interest to dozens of these people in puberty — boys and girls who formed strong attachments to everything in sight. All objects drew them — especially the vélo, the thirty year old Ronson Varaflame lighter, the miniature pocket radio. I elected to give in: a clear case of force majeur. There were comings and goings all the time, and their vivacious energy and sheer exuberance kept them going non-stop until well after the hour of nightfall in camp. They yielded only when Madame's husband arrived in a furious temper triggered by my neighbours' complaints. He roared and they went.

As the days passed, the vélo would disappear for hours on end which gave me some anxiety. There would be long noisy arguments outside the tent every day as to whose turn it was to ride my beloved bicycle. I knew that I should, and could, have been stern about all this and that it would have been better if I had closed down this anarchic youth club. But there were no leaders to deal with — just an unruly, unmalicious, pubescent soviet. No formalities accompanied their visitations, and I came to dread the rasping sounds of the outer tent zips that ought to have broken many pulls before. But by now I was in lassitude and let a great laziness, a mood of absolute laissez-faire take over. I worked hard at the art of doing nothing. I even fretted less about the vélo, and the valuables in the zip pockets of the priceless anorak. I wanted to make no demands; even more, I wished none to be made of me.

However, as I watched the whirlwind behaviour of these joyous, uncontrolled youths, the idea of invoicing their parents presented itself. I recalled my own teenage spent at a school in a North Devon wilderness during the war years. It was a small place for a hundred and sixty boarders divided into four Houses. Mine was Grenville, the others being Brereton (after the Founder), Courtenay and Fortescue. My number was one three eight. R.F. Delderfield had been there and *To Serve Them All My Days* was the story of his own time at West Buckland — Bamfylde in the book, the name of a clump of trees five miles away on Exmoor.

Would these maddeningly boisterous, but totally unobjectionable youngsters, have enjoyed, and benefited from, such an upbringing on the fringes of wild moorland? From a life where there was little choice — compulsory sport of all kinds, rugger above all (which the fifteen a side game was then in England called) cricket and cross country running; and where small new boys were beaten by prefects for having jam on their faces (when the fortnight's school rule grace period was up) during their first lost and frightened days; and when the most weighty rite was to muffle the sound of homesickness after 'lights out' in the dormitory?

We spent several more days at this campsite in the Vendee filling them with long solitary walks, and resting with a second reading of Patrick Cosgrave's *Lives of Enoch Powell*. On July 14th, Bastille Day, the countryside for miles around was alight with the sparkle of annual fireworks. The days usually ended with the youngsters shouting their heads off as we played deafening pontoon — vingt et un. We came nowhere close to agreement about the laws of this card game. Once, with the help of Bernard Shaw, I pierced their preoccupied minds by quoting the Shavian view of their age group. "What a fine thing is youth. What a pity that it has to be wasted on the young."

"Merde," (merde: the 's' word in English) they all yelled. "Merde, merde, merde."

Nevertheless, I was touchingly impressed by their reaction when I announced one morning, an hour before departure, that it was time to get going again.

Chapter Seven

It was a good fast run to Avrilée where we put up at a hotel on the main road, and where the dining-room was about a quarter full with whispering people.

The weather was now unpleasantly hot, and the roadwork, even on fairly level ground, thirst making. We stopped often to deal with this, but only where draught beer was pulled. There was serious interest in our odyssey wherever we hydrated. Earlier it had been, "To Spain? By bicycle? Alone?" and heads shook in disbelief. But now it was "From Roscoff? By bicycle? Alone?", with eyebrows arching high. I was curious about the reasons for this fascination, and presumed it was less to do with the vélo and distance — more with my solitary state. The word 'solitaire' was more sobbed than spoken. "Vous êtes solitaire, Monsieur?" or "Vous êtes tout en seul?" as might be asked of one in mourning. I deduced that the French find solitude strange.

The traffic, as we approached the region of Les Sables d'Olonne, was becoming denser by the hour. The driving, and nationalities did not distinguish themselves, was aggressive and impatient. Here was a long, visually endless beach stretching farther than the sands of Blackpool, Southend and Bournemouth laid end to end. I hoped to reach La Rochelle that night bound for the Île de Ré which had been highly recommended by a GP friend of ours. The island was some five kilometres offshore linked to the mainland by a mountainous bridge; but I did not plan to cross it that night. The approach to La Rochelle was draining, nerve-racking, on the fast, danger filled road. The roaring noise of cars, lorries, and fast moving motor homes made me very tense. I kept close, sometimes unwisely so, to the very edge of the dual carriage-way with its deep trench on the side. At last the bridge came into view on the horizon, and whereas I had been told that it looked like a mountain to scale and come down, to me it resembled a roller coaster rising to its summit over the sea.

It was early in the hot evening when we reached the end of the land but I was too tired and agitated after the day's eighty kilometre run to attempt the rise and fall of the traverse in fading light. I decided to lodge on the mainland, have a good sleep and then, fresh, to take on the bridge in the morning. I was surprised at the charges I saw while circling the lane entrances — ten pounds and more for a four wheel vehicle each way; but only a tenth of that for vélos.

It took over two hours to find a bar with rooms at twelve pounds a night. While riding and searching, I saw a dead dog in the roadside ravine, carelessly killed, carefully thrown. It looked like a pure bred German Shepherd, and I supposed that the colliding motorist would have said that (in the situation) he had to choose, in a split second, between the life of the dog or ten human beings.

We found the square in a run down neighbourhood where there were two bars. Only one of them had rooms to let. The Patron showed me to the only one available which we reached after long mazey walks upstairs and through passageways. This room was not unlike the one taken by Mr and Mrs Henry Root in Paris, except that while I had a lavabo and shower, the WC was on yet another floor — a labyrinthine walk away. But I was tired and nervous, hungry and thirsty, and consequently grateful to come to any kind of rest at all. Although the magic plastic money card signs were not displayed, I asked Monsieur if la carte bleu (Visa) would be acceptable. His 'Non' was emphatic. After I had paid him in cash for the room, I had fifteen francs left. This allowed me to have a small glass of beer and I appreciated the complimentary peanuts — dinner that night. My host's dark face was scarred, his menacing moustaches drooped, his expression, angry; but he must have been a bit soft in heart as well. Only he knew about my cash flow problem. Only he could have told a drinker at the bar that I was broke. This man owned a café nearby, and offered me dinner on the slate until bank time in the morning. I acknowledged his trusting kindness, but declined the offer thinking that a dinnerless day would harm me not at all. Then I told myself that I had just enjoyed a filling nut cutlet.

In the room there were fleas, bed bugs, and mosquitoes. From next door, thinly walled, an eccentric martial neighbour made loud, military noises all through the night. He drilled and marched until dawn, when reveille ended night ops on the parade ground, and from his bugle of a hooter great snoring commenced. He had been very much the Regimental Sergeant Major on the barrack square. Surely I was hearing from Beau Geste incarnate. These orders were clear and loud echoes from Sidi bel Abbes itself. He shunned, stood at ease, called for right markers, about turned, sloped, presented, and ported arms. He wheeled to right and left and rebuked a soldier for being idle on parade. He eyes lefted, eyes righted, and took the general salute. He slow marched, and quick marched, he did his bayonet drill and must have slain single-handedly an entire enemy platoon. Now and then he praised his troops. "Well done, men."

Early on, I had decided to enjoy the free entertainment next door, foregoing sleep that night in La Rochelle. After a hilarious visit to the WC, at about four in the morning (this facility, with all its design faults and technical short-comings, would have been perfect in a Whitehall farce) I fell to an uncontrollable laughing fit. In noise level it matched, if it did not outdo, the commands, reprimands, and pep talks next door. I worried that the Legionnaire on hearing this, after a stand easy order for instance, would think that he and his unit were being debunked. I feared that he might order an attack on my door, and open up a second front. The more I tried to suppress it, the louder did I laugh. Luckily the volume of his do or die commands rose to a Horseguards crescendo as he halted his troops for the last time, and landed on his bed by freefall, sheet made, parachute.

The late and legendary R.S.M. Brittan would have been pleased with this tartar for discipline next door. Once, in the course of this impossible night, I remembered the occasion when I met the famous Coldstream Guardsman aboard the Bell's whisky Thames Barge. He was in his eightieth year, acting as official greeter, striking in a long crimson brass buttoned coat. Every hair of his full, white moustache was in its proper place. He talked entertainingly on a hot summer night, moored to the Barbican in Plymouth. He told me that he wanted to take his battalion's (based in Germany at the time) parade on his eightieth birthday. The request was turned down.

Morning had broken, and I had just enough change for a small cup of coffee after which I cycled around filling time, waiting for the business day to start. In a neighbouring suburb I found a branch of the Credit Mutuel Bank. One of the cashiers reacted nervously when I reached down for the holdall on the floor containing the valuables. My movements must have been too jerky. But she helped me with the card machine, and although shattered and wounded from many bedroom bites, I vowed to storm and conquer the bridge to the Île de Ré.

In these parts, there were more and more 'piste cyclable' signs, and taking one, we rode with a father and his three children who, with pleasant conversation, led us to the bridge. Ducking under the pay barrier (my guide told me that it simply was not done for cyclists to pay) we began the ascent — and thought we should never reach the summit. It was a kind of psychological capitulation, but at last we rolled down to the Island where there was flattish land and plenty of 'piste cyclables'.

Some nine kilometres from the bridge, we came upon a large campsite-cum-hotel. We checked into a luxurious ground floor en suite room. Then I indulged myself by passing expensive, lotus eating days. Nearby was a late and noisy disco night-club, and the operators advertised their special nightly attractions by driving slowly around the campsite with headlines like 'GIRLS CE SOIR' on the sides of the truck.

The easy days passed, and at the end of every one I told myself that we must move on in the morning, but it took almost a fortnight to summon the necessary will. I knew that this particular stop was lasting too long. The weather was hot, and I spent the time on gentle rides with vélo, and many hours on various beaches. At one, people wore various bathing costume, or none at all. It was all casual and relaxed — the dressed and the undressed appearing to have no interest whatever in each others' preferences; free, easy, and comfortable.

These beaches were relatively empty until about four pm, when the whole world, tout le monde, arrived in sprawling family gangs with turbulent children and dogs. They would stay until well after eight o'clock, when all the good things in boxes and plastic bags had been consumed. Top dog on one beach was a jet black Doberman Pinscher called, phonetically, Pee-Jee. His owners were a sun-loving couple — au naturel. He was dark haired with a pony tail; she, brown, with long blonde hair. One day when it was time to go, Pee-Jee was not ready. He obviously had unfinished business to complete with about fifty other dogs, and wanted more time for this purpose. He easily eluded Madame, still naked, several times. She looked all set to break local sprinting-on-sand records. Monsieur, now fully dressed and standing on top of the dune, directed the chase. Once when Pee-Jee sold a dummy that would have brought Twickenham to its feet, he let out as memorable an O la la as one will ever hear. It was impossible to know whether he was moved pridefully by Pee-Jee's jinking form, or exasperated by his lady's poor tackling.

This was a hedonistic time; and while there was a spasm or two of shame and regret concerning this prolonged skive, I liked it so much that I put off departure day repeatedly — abetted by a model receptionist who told me that it was essential, obligatory, for me to do exactly what I wanted to do, and that the world should mind its own business. I told this beauty that she was a wise person. One who cared not a fig, moreover, whether I would get to Santander or not.

Petit déjeuner was served in a geodesic structure made of heat-giving transparent material, and the room's temperature kept coffee hot for a long time. The sun rayed in and boiled us all. The waitresses were mature, cheerful and charming: I relished our morning persiflage. It was hard to leave all this — but one day I came within a few centimetres of leaving — for good.

It was a Sunday morning and we were going well and safely to the seaward end of the island. The traffic was intense. There were never more than one or two seconds between the overtaking vehicles whose drivers, mainly, were giving me good space. Sometimes when riding, my hands overlap the outside of the vélo's handlebar grips. There is no particular reason for doing this, but it was as well that, when a big fast, grey car glanced the left hand grip with its doors, my fingers were just in board. Had the vehicle at that speed hit my hand, I would have lost control and been killed.

The car slowed, pulled off the road and stopped. I kept going, neither hurt nor shocked. As I realised that this incident had taken no immediate toll, I expected that there would be delayed reaction in minutes, hours, or days: but the condition never did set in. The driver came running towards me.

He was middle-aged, balding and wore thick glasses over a dark bushy moustache. The man was in a panic, and was quickly joined by his attractive blonde wife. Their two teenage children, boy and girl, stayed in the back seat of the car which I noticed had French number plates – the nationality I feared least on the road. They looked afraid, and the driver was shaking as he spoke. "Are you hurt? Are you badly hurt?" he could not think properly. I had, after all, ridden two hundred metres since the impact – and now at our roadside meeting he looked imploringly for reassurance that I was all right. Images of police, a court case, perhaps a massive insurance claim were racing across his mind and he became incoherent in his torment.

I showed him my left hand, and explained that he had not made contact with it – only with the (undamaged) handlebar. This gave him indescribable relief and gradually, although still trembling, he calmed down and apologised many times. His lady smiled sweetly at me, and slowly they walked back, arm in arm to their car. As I went on my way, we waved and I saw him fumbling with a cigarette packet.

Some four or five kilometres farther on I heard the gentle toot of a car horn. This time they nearly killed themselves. So eager was he on this overtake to give me the maximum possible space that the car ended up on the wrong side of the road – all four occupants looking intently at me. But for a loud and sustained pressing on the horn of the fast oncoming

71

car, there would have been a fatal head-on collision. Then I waited for my own post shock trembling to start — thankfully, in vain.

We carried on and I patted the handlebar grips thinking about thin tassels, half seconds and a couple of centimetres. Afterwards, and wickedly, I thought about a base opportunity one would have had to act out the gross lie of serious injury. In a flash, I returned to a real accident, self brought in 1981, when I too drove a car — drunk and into an uncomplaining hedge.

At the campsite/hotel I was on a demi pension arrangement, and looked forward to a late and well made dinner every night served by a young and nubile girl of Turkish origin. While the room I had was spacious — large enough for the vélo as well — and with a good private bathroom and all those facilities, there was no refrigerator. Rather than go to the bother of asking the management to put large and relatively cheap bottles of Kanterbrau (La Grande Blonde, bought in the site's own supermarket) in their cold storage, I drank them at happy hour in room high temperature with peanuts. This allowed me to appreciate all the more the perfectly chilled carafes of Muscadet later, much later, at table.

In the evening of the car impact day, I told the waitress, as usual, about my adventures. On hearing about this close call, she expressed surprise that I appeared to be unaffected by it. I told her as well about the sand in my left eye that had been troubling me for a couple of days, and which had been blown on to the eyeball by frequently strong, warm winds. She fetched a clean white, stiffly starched napkin, and in the gentlest way tried to remove the tiny grains. The result of this kindly act on her part was immediate. Hungry customers raised brows over their own untroubled eyes, wondering when normal service — always on the slow side — would resume. She dislodged two crystals but said that she could see more, and suggested expert treatment. Sometimes I was bothered by the irritation, sometimes not, and hoped that tears, optimistically of laughter — if not, of the other sort — would flush out the trouble.

The waitress went back to her work explaining my

problem, in some detail, to customers. The news particularly interested a gentleman and his lady dining two tables away. I speculated that he may have been an eye specialist, or a chiropodist. He was difinitely interested in feet — and quite keenly on those of Madame sitting opposite him. He de-flip-flopped her and himself with quick finesse. With his now bare feet under the table, and comfortably placed over hers, he drew eyes with a fork on the smoothed linen tablecloth.

After dinner, and happy at midnight, I decided to try the nearby disco. Next morning I realised just how mentally abandoned I must have been in choosing to go to that place. My normal attitude to this sort of entertainment is such that I would willingly go into debt if that was the only way to avoid it. At six pounds for the smallest beer bottle I had ever seen, with headache making lights, and damaging eardrum noise, I savoured the peace that would come in a few minutes on the fresh air side of the heavy, Praetorian guarded, door.

The 'can do' attitude of bicycle repair man in France (mainly called Peugeot) was pleasing me very much. Front wheel wobble? No problem. Broken spokes? Easy. In 1991 the charge for this kind of work was around the three pounds mark: bicycle repair man Peugeot seems ready to serve in every town. As a 'no can do' person myself, I found this practically and psychologically invaluable, knowing, as I had been told so many times, that there would inevitably be considerable wear and tear on the vélo in the course of a ride like ours.

Broken spoke, and front wheel wobble work, had been done on the far end of the island at La Couarde. The weather on the day was not good; and wind blasted and gusted hard. The rain started and stopped, the clouds came, went, and returned after the rain. We set course on the piste cyclable by the seashore en route to Saint Martin de Ré, the capital. The left eye, as we rode, felt clear and comfortable but on approaching the town I saw hospital signs, and large notices asking for quiet in the vicinity. It was a big light grey coloured building and I followed the Casualty (D'urgence) arrows. Time did not matter. I was prepared for a crowded waiting-room and for hours to pass before being called.

d

Two people were in the large, light, well-appointed, flower arranged waiting-room. There were no benches — instead, roomy armchairs with ashtrays to hand. Forty-five minutes passed quickly and agreeably. While waiting, a man came in, trying with both hands to hold on to his back. He was in pain and I tried to console him by saying that it simply happened to be his turn — that everyone did their backs in, and that it was only a matter of when, not if, the crick was felt. This made him feel better, and I demonstrated the pre-emptive over rotation exercise. Then I was taken to a treatment room.

Two ladies in white stood ready to help — a doctor and a nurse. The former wore trousers, was tanned, young with dark hair, and tantalisingly beautiful. After examination, when I was told that there were more than ten grains of sand in the eye, a stinging douche was poured on it, and I braced, steeling myself for what was to come. I had already seen sharp instruments being sterilised by the nurse, and trembled at the thought of them making contact with the surface of the eye.

The enchantingly lovely doctor put her left hand on my cheek — and I knew how I would get through. Fantasy saved me. I was not in a French hospital casualty ward any more. Her hands were gloveless, and the flesh of her slender brown fingers touched my face. She caressed me as we picnicked by a deserted river bank on a perfect day, a blanket on the ground, a bottle in the cool, flowing water. And she gazed deeply, lovingly, longingly, lastingly, into my left eye.

In her office she wrote out a prescription for ointment. She had already secured an eye patch around my head which she told me to wear for twenty-four hours. She was a casualty specialist, and this work cost two hundred and forty-eight francs — about twenty-five pounds. I did not have this amount on me and probably could not have paid for the ointment either. I offered to sign an I.O.U. but they said that was unnecessary. I then behaved badly and well. I tore up the cream prescription, and removed the eye patch on reaching the roads, knowing that I would have been a one-eyed danger in the saddle. I rode back quickly to my quarters

for cash, and settled the bill. They liked this at the hospital —
they were not expecting me until the next day.

After this overlong stay on the Île de Ré I paid the big
account, and left for the bridge, mainland, and more southerly
progress. As the bridge came in sight, I felt the onset of a
road panic attack. This sensation had recurred a few times
when driving cars on motorways. Caused by morbid mental
figments (imaginary crashing, falling, losing control) these
anxiety spasms cause alarm. You are about to die. You feel
dizzy, unbalanced, and ask yourself whether the last breath
will come in seconds, or minutes. The only way to manage
these frightening periods I have found, is to stop, to get off,
or to get out. And then to think of something else. I have
never troubled to discuss this personal phenomenon with an
expert — believing it to be psychosomatically driven, fed by
redundant worry and passing pessimism.

Chapter Eight

I dismounted just before the summit of the bridge, and instead of looking at a map or doing something useful, I watched the wrong things: the sea – a Niagara Fall below, and the traffic roaring to and fro. This made the condition worse, and I spent half an hour doubting if I could remount and carry on. I tried all the tricks – desperately seeking subjects, people and events that would divert me from thinking about the world to come – if there was one.

Then, feeling as woozy as I had ever done, I walked the vélo to the summit and looked at the great arc of the ominous steel structure. Swallowing and gasping, and gulping for air, I could only think about the traffic jams that would soon build up as ambulances or hearses or helicopters screamed and hovered and winched the cause away. And what of the vélo? Would they take care, and ship it safely back to Plymouth? How would the news of my sudden death reach home? Should I wait to die any longer – or carry vélo over the side barrier and let it go and then follow – or should I cling onto it, so that we could fall and drown together? And by the way, was it true that with drowning comes a high speed film of your life to date?

With hands shaking, I unzipped the right side back pocket on the rear pannier, and took out my cigarette rolling tobacco pouch with the old Ronson lighter. Three times I dropped them and three times did I try to roll up, but fingers were so unsteady that this regularly pleasant and creative task was beyond me. Without the solace of a smoke I concentrated hard on the subject of drowning. Would the agony of final breathlessness be worse than now? Would oblivion come

76

before, or after, the last struggle for air?

At my request, the film rolled. It was screened at normal speed, faithfully episodic, beginning with childhood in the Punjab of Raj days, riding the pony Araminta in early morning heat. The seven-year-old — wrestling with Eton collar studs at a boarding school in Cornwall. The next place in North Devon, and boils bursting after falling on the ball. Reunion with parents after five years of war separation in India; nervous apprehension about the prospect of meeting them again; of having to get to know, and to get on with, two strangers.

The first ship in Middlesborough and the career years at sea finished by mild myopia. Searching then for something to do, unqualified, on land. The labouring at an electric tool factory in Slough. A stevedoring job in Montreal. Playing tennis there with a beautiful brunette girl of Dutch origin in tormenting white shorts. Marriage. The birth of a baby girl. Her leukaemia and death in Montreal aged three years and ten months. Then two baby boys. The start of work in local commercial radio. 'The British Half Hour', an idea sold to a cinema chain sponsor and progress from that to open line radio shows, and various television series. The return to Britain in 1972 for the start of local commercial radio in the UK. Plymouth — as Programme Controller of Plymouth Sound, the city's first own radio station. Weekend work in London at the same time with the capital's news station LBC. Eight day weeks. The wearying wars with the IBA (Independent Broadcasting Authority) and resignation in 1982. Radio Devon and Radio Cornwall in 1983 with 'Afternoon Sou'West' for the BBC. 1984 — Cancer, Dracula and Nell Gwynne. The goodness of people at that time, and the reshuffling of priorities.

Nothing in this kaleidoscope, however, could take me away. I still stood giddily holding onto the bridge for another hour, and convinced myself that with all balance and will lost, I probably could not even wheel vélo for the rest of the way downhill. The end of my world was near. I put both hands up to my ears to shut out noise and torture, resembling perhaps Edvard Munch's 'The Scream'. At that moment, and without reason, I thought of a fat farm near Ipswich where

77

I had been an inmate for ten days in 1978. My aim had been to render off at least a stone in weight, and to release what a knowledgeable well wisher had called "a dangerous, highly coiled, spring." It worked. The first five days on nothing but lemon water. Beating the ex-army PT Instructor ('Rod' as in Laver to his friends) every day on the tennis court. Endless themes of food — the sole topic of talk with fellow volunteer detainees — all of us bound together by common bonds of self-indulgence and not a little narcissism. If, I rationalised in my psychologically seized up state on this bridge, I could beat 'Rod Laver' (younger, thinner and fitter) on lemon water while he cruelly announced that he had prepared on his girlfriend's steak and kidney pie, roast beef and Yorkshire pudding, then surely I could now find enough spunk to ride the vélo. Had I at last found the potency of auto-suggestion? I jumped on and we were off on a sixty kilometre ride that day with no more deathly dread of heart failure, stroke, fainting, or collapse.

Our destinations, as we cleared the complicated streets and roads of La Rochelle were Rochefort for St. Agnan. We travelled well and uneventfully for several hours. Ahead, and at a great distance in this flattish country, there was an even bigger and more threatening mountain of a bridge. If the Île de Ré span was Alpine, the one to come was Himalayan. From afar it looked a bridge much too high for us. Beating 'Rod Laver' by lemon water again drove us on, and we cheerfully challenged this perfectly formed, hump backed bully, won the match, and came down very fast on the other side of its zenith.

Accommodation was increasingly difficult to find by this time as the French holiday season started to peak. In St. Agnan I was directed to 'Camping Chambres' at what had been a working farm. Mosquitoes, flies and bed bugs (familiar companions) were everywhere in charge — their rule, ruthless. After a disappointing dinner I discovered that I would be lying on a sloping mattress. After patchy, scratchy and painful sleep, we left early with nothing inside but the taste of toothpaste. We rode smoothly through empty countryside in the early morning, drooling about café au lait and croissants. It was not a happy start. I itched and sneezed for a long time without benefit of early warnings, and feared losing control. I decided to pause and have (even enjoy) a good get-it-over-and-done-with session but the skin and nasal irritations persisted — until I ceased believing in their existence. I willed them away, so that I could dream and salivate over the steaming bowl and fresh buttered crusty hunk, or even better, a sandwich jambon beurre. Then we passed the gate of a pig farm just as I had been slobbering on phantom ham. The farmer waved and shouted "Bonjour." I replied; we carried on. A few more metres, and thirst and hunger took over. We returned to the gate where the farmer was still in sight. He waved us in, and soon I was seated at a huge kitchen table in a big untidy room with Madame at the coffee pot, and ham sandwich board.

After a life-saving breakfast, the farmer showed me round his intensive food production establishment. Five thousand pigs were housed in hangar-like buildings with automatic temperature and other environmental controls. Proudly he took me to 'La maternité' where several sows were nursing their litters — on average, thirteen piglets. He spoke at length about his 'cochons', quite unsentimentally. He seemed a little puzzled at my reaction when at the door of one 'maternité' compartment I saw a tiny dead pig.

"C'est mort?" I asked.

"Oui, oui c'est mort," he confirmed, still-born.

I asked how old the siblings were and he said three weeks. Their little lifeless brother or sister had been with them all the time, and I wondered what effect this would have on them and their mother, but decided not to ask. After the tour we returned to the farmhouse for more coffee, tobacco and talk, and I was surprised that we had been there for over two hours. I thanked my hosts for their goodness, and now properly refuelled, we resumed our expedition. Next would come Royan and a car ferry across the Gironde — avoiding Bordeaux.

We bucked a strong, hot head wind all the way to Royan — suffocatingly full of holiday making people from many nations. I looked for banks and those unfathomable cash dispensers. Perhaps it was wrong to worry so much about robbery. Without this uneasiness, I would have drawn more at each heart stopping swallow of the plastic with its arrow, metal strip, embossed number, and secret PIN.

It was now about one in the afternoon and banks were closed. I was too unsure and afraid to take on the cash machinery alone; always I asked for supervision, which was never refused. British voices and GB plates were everywhere. Tired after head winds, and hilly going, I abandoned the attempt to draw cash in this crowded place, and concentrated on finding the ferry.

The Gironde crossing cost about two pounds fifty and took forty minutes. On this vessel, vehicles roll on and off through the ship's sides. On maps, the gap of water looks to be more than seven kilometres — the distance given by a cafeteria assistant. On reaching Le Verdon at about 2 pm, I concentrated on getting cash.

I looked for the signs of wizardry — Visa and Access. In the tourist office near the ferry terminal, I was told that the bank Crédit Agricole would do nicely. I found the branch with some difficulty, having been misdirected a few times, or perhaps I had not properly understood the instructions. Inside the small room it was stiflingly hot and crowded. I was sweating heavily as I joined the shortest queue. People on both sides of the counter were doing business at a maddeningly slow pace, and I was hot and bothered.

At last Madame and I could eyeball each other. She had blonde coloured hair, was of an uncertain age and Boadicean presence. On that day she was not pleased with the human race. All around her were Romans. I smiled solicitously and even thought about a wink, but realised in the nick of time that an attempt at intimacy would have been unwise. Then, like a novice conjuror, unsure as to whether he should have taken up magic late in life, I slowly dealt her the two cards. One by one. First, Visa: no reaction. Next, after a breath holding pause, I played my one remaining card: Access. Forehead sweat plopped on it. Again, Madame did not respond. She waited, savouring the moment to come. She began to make her move. First she swung her head from side to side almost imperceptibly. The shakings increased in speed until at the end she might have been watching a long tennis rally at the net filmed in Charlie Chaplin's early days. At last came the orgasm.

"Non, non, non Monsieur. Ce n'est pas possible. CE N'EST PAS POSSIBLE."

I contemplated suicide. I looked away from the flushed face in the afterglow of her climax — resenting this selfish, one way intercourse that had brought her to rapture. With as sombre an expression as I could compose, I asked her to direct me to the nearest bank where my cards might have some hope of a welcome. She named a town. It was sixty kilometres away. For the second time that day, the earth moved for her. And it was not yet three in the afternoon.

On the way to Soulac-sur-Mer, the next place south, and some ten kilometres down the road, I became angry with me. In self-hatred, I put this question to the vélo. "Why didn't this fool upon your saddle take the trouble beforehand to arrange a better way of getting cash? Why didn't the idiot organise Eurocheques, travellers' cheques and things like that?"

The vélo answered, "Such properly ordered and prepared people would not be doing what you are doing with and to me in the first place."

"Bull's-eye, vélo," I shouted, and changed the subject.

I was beginning to learn about the warfare of high season continental holiday making. Most people, I concluded, must like being in, and part of, dense crowds. So full was Soulac-sur-Mer, that it was impossible to wheel, let alone ride, the bicycle. Everywhere we turned there was nerve jarring hub-bub. There was neither space nor peace, and I had but centimes in the back pocket of my shorts. I felt like a Trappist in Southend-on-Sea facing August Bank Holiday.

Putting the features in bogus, casual mode, I looked in the narrow streets heaving with humanity for signs of money — 'Banque', 'Crédit', 'Visa', 'Access'. Anything. There was nothing. I chafed at being broke, and having nowhere to sleep as the dusky overcast closed in. Life was hellish that early evening, and I recited over and over again Pope's line. 'This long disease, my life.' I was totally fed up, troubled and alienated. This was the lowest low so far. After half an hour of slow motion, weaving like a snail through the body jams, and apologising every few seconds for running into members

81

of this mad mill, I joined a long queue at a place where money was changing hands. When it was my turn at the counter, patient Madame said that I could use my 'carte' in the machine outside which characteristically, I had not seen. I joined this even longer line up, and after another vexing wait, with eyes fixed on the parked vélo, I was there. The technology and I squared up to each other. I bowed and scraped a bit, and inserted the card. It cursed furiously in several languages — in my own, in huge lettering, it spat out the insult — 'TRANSACTION ABORTED'. The Visa was, sans doute, persona non grata here and the rabid, maddened engine puked the plastic out. I was ready to wipe bloodstains off it.

A few metres, which meant minutes in time away, I saw, as a shipwrecked mariner will see a lifeboat, the sign 'Carte Bleu'. Visa. Another queue, another arrival at the keyhole of mammon's storehouse. Behind me was a pleasant, placid looking middle-aged woman. I asked her for help. She knew exactly what to do, and wanted to know how much money I needed. I settled for sixteen hundred francs. She looked away bashfully as I pressed the buttons with the secret PIN digits. After a little wait there came the sound of brief, comfortable, whirring intestinal exhalations, and the monster slowly evacuated the notes.

Feeling more secure, we got out of Soulac-sur-Mer and had a fast run in failing light to Montalivet, the sea close on our right. Although hot, the road and wind conditions were good. We pulled up at a hotel on the beach and going into the bar, saw a prop forward of a mature woman bouncing a young man, wearing a leather jacket, out of the premises; booted, a brace of battered haversacks followed him. Two German Shepherd dogs slept in the entrance. They, and the many heavyweight male drinkers at the bar ignored the scene. Puzzled, I asked the daughter of the house about this as she washed and polished glasses. "Why aren't the dogs at least assisting Maman?" I enquired. "And what about that massive reserve power sitting on bar stools?"

She explained that this was a regular occurrence, and a personal pleasure for her mother who always enjoyed, looked forward to, the arrival of banned Georges. He came from a rich and well known family who had chucked him out, but with a great deal of money, which he spent wherever he could in bars and, let it be whispered, possibly, just possibly, on drugs as well. The daughter said that he would probably return. Maman, I was informed, was a lover of le rugby and on visiting days usually managed three push-over scores against Georges.

He did come back a few minutes later with his luggage and swayed slowly to the bar. "Maman," the daughter called quietly to her mother, who ran on, eyes agleam, and with a few self-psyching snorts, got the scrummage going at once. Her set piece forward power was awesome, and there was no contest. Having loose head advantage she touched him down outside between the door posts, and scored twice more − a conversion from a place kick with one bag, and a half volley dropped goal with the other.

"Bravo. Vive le rugby," I said, and Madame, modest in victory, melted.

Her daughter wanted to practice English with me. Obliging, I said, "Your hotel is of course full. Yes? Then would you, perhaps, have a shed or garage where I could put down my sleeping-bag and bivouac?"

She left to consult with Papa at the other end of the bar. He was as little as his lady was large, with darting eyes full of the signs of cash flow. I heard him say 'caravan' and he explained that he had a spare one at the back. This was wonderful news, and as there was no rush, and because I was in funds again, I insisted that we all celebrate this luck, and Madame's forward play, over a drink. I had not been expecting an offer of self-contained private luxury. Half an hour later I contentedly wheeled vélo behind him, as he showed us to our night's rest.

We picked our way through a yard full of fowl and fish bones, and other dog teased refuse, to the caravan: or to something that when new, might have been called that. It was battered, partially roofless and had palpably been used for years as a lopsided rubbish tip full of rotting mattresses, stinking pillows, broken chairs and other items which made all but the tiniest movement impossible.

Leaving vélo outside, I tried to level things out a bit, but was really hoping that after dinner, tiredness, food and drink would take me to oblivion. Morpheus after Bacchus. To help these Gods, I drank two bottles of dry white wine in the hot crowded restaurant. To my right, a loving couple had ordered crab and lobster. He was having a lot more bother with the surgery than his deftly fingered girl, and this had been observed by a matronly table neighbour. She left her own food, and skilfully mined the flesh from the young man's seafood. He flushed a little, thanked his helper and was not diminished, outwardly, in his loved one's eyes. Diners came and went. Papa, by now in fast perpetual motion, cleared and laid tables with the speed of a supermarket prize winner filling a trolley in sixty seconds.

After a small coffee and large cognac, I went for a long walk on the everlasting beach, hoping to tire out even more in advance of the night's arrangements; but I could not stop worrying about the worsening rear wheel wobble of which I had been conscious when leaving St Agnan. All seemed in order mechanically: again, at one motor garage I had asked Madame to watch me as I rode around the forecourt. Could she see this wobble which I could feel?

"Un peu," she reported. "Un petit peu. Pas grave. Pas de probleme."

I was not convinced, and believed that we had a potentially serious matter to deal with. In this flat, oyster and sunflower country, we were doing, sometimes by our standards, very high speeds, and as I walked with the torch on the dark deserted beach that night, dread images of the back wheel leaving us at thirty-five kilometres per hour came easily. I could not get this out of my mind. Yet the axle nuts were sound. At last I stopped thinking about it, mentally snuggling the advice about trouble. 'Never trouble trouble 'til trouble troubles you.' That would have to do. We would stop at the next cycle garage we saw.

Sitting on a comfortable rock near the water's edge, and listening to the fade of the sea's voice on the ebbing tide, I rolled a final cigarette foreseeing that it would be folly to smoke in my leaning hovel on sunken wheels. I had noticed, but could not move, a heavy, leaking, reeking container of paint stripper close to where my head would have to stay

84

put. I was not concerned about fume inhalation – there was a wide ventilating shaft overhead where part of the roof did not exist.

The roll up was drawing well. Considering the darkness, I had made a good one and felt, as ever, grateful to the tobacco that had given me life support for so long. I declaimed from Jane Austen's *Mansfield Park* and her reference to the weed (in a quotation of a quotation) from that book. 'Blest leaf whose aromatic gales dispense – to the Templar, modesty – to the Parson, sense.'

Soon after I had started walking back, and fearful of the night to come, the rain came. Slowly and in huge drops at first, then torrentially. A great thunderstorm began its overture for a son et lumière show of devastating noise and blinding light. Counting the seconds between the lightning and thunder, I estimated that the storm's centre was some fifteen miles away. I was quickly drenched and cold. The tobacco in my faithful old pouch would not be usable for many hours. I splashed my way back to the caravan. The contents in the four non-waterproof panniers on the vélo were soaked. On this overnight stop there was no separate shelter for vélo – and little to choose between conditions inside and outside this wretched thing on flat, buried tyres.

The storm went on all night and there was no cover anywhere. By now the hotel had been long closed. There was no night porter. A dry refuge inside the locked door was barred to us. There was neither porch nor canopy. I spent the hours until daybreak, and clearing sky, now squatting, now lying, in various places in and out of, and sometimes underneath, this ghastly, rotting, waterlogged hulk decaying on mud and sand. It was a horrible, shivering, sleepless night and I was in control of nothing.

Every few minutes I walked to the front door of the hotel. I craved teeth cleaning water and the flush of the cistern. When eventually a sleepy man unlocked the main entrance, I launched into the story of my night, expecting him to be spellbound. He was as responsive as a commuter hearing a delayed train announcement.

In the narrow, awkward, WC, there was a time-switch light which cut out at a humiliatingly inconvenient moment.

Unluckily, my lighter was by the washbasin next door, and having entered the cubicle with the light already on, I could not find the switch control. After a few unsuccessful passes and prods on the walls in total darkness, I gave up and cast myself as the star of a one man high farce hit. First a chuckle, then giggles: soon the full belly blasting range. And the let loose laughter went on and on and on. This drew quick attention and interest. There was an angry banging on the door, "What's wrong? Who's there? What's going on?" the vexed patronne wanted to know. Perchance she thought that Georges had gained some of her ground. She asked for him by name. I could only splutter and gasp that I was not Georges, that I was the Anglais à vélo and that I was now in a situation 'délicat et intime' and could not see to function properly. And then there was light. The switch was on the wall outside. I recovered, brushed the teeth and shaved badly with a water damaged razor nearly out of power. Momentarily, I gave the tedium of daily humdrum life a good mark with its dryness, visible light switches and bathroom conveniences.

We left Montalivet in hot drying sunshine bound for the next stop at Plage Carcans. On this leg I did a study of the way motorists from different countries gave me, or did not give me, good space when overtaking. On the stretch between Montalivet and Carcans my league table (Friends of the Vélo) was topped by F (France) followed by NL (Holland), D (Germany), B (Belgium), CH (Switzerland), IRL (Ireland, I (Italy) and GB (Great Britain). My fellow countrymen came bottom, I wanted to think, not because they suffer from vélophobia; but are more anxious about driving on the other side of the road, with a consequently greater fear of head-on collisions. This would, of course, also be true of IRL, above GB: maybe there are more vélophiles in their country than in ours. But it was not a GB plated car that had so very nearly killed me on the Île de Ré. That car was marked F. F for top score.

We were making fast time on this good, flat road, even though the rear wheel was wobbling more and more. I tried not to think about it (we had yet to see a vélo garage) and to shut out of my ears and mind the sound of traffic roar.

Vehicles volleyed and thundered by in both directions. Instead, I tried to work out by some coarse formula, long since forgotten, how many times I would have been overtaken between Roscoff and Santander. The number was half a million. Exactly. That was the figure. "Exactly half a million?" I queried, "Precisely five hundred thousand?" The computer confirmed that this was so. "Not a car more – not a caravan nor a lorry less." The count has never been challenged.

On this stretch, we saw many families on cycling holidays, confidently carrying their small children on specially designed pillion seats. Once I saw a young and pretty mother riding well: suspended from her neck in a kind of sling, slept her baby. The infant's head protruded from the pouch type carrier, much like a tiny kangaroo. As we passed, Maman was singing a lullaby in French.

Plage Carcans, like all the seaside places on our way, was noisy, hot and crowded. There were many Britons, and we were surrounded by them at our first beer stop of the day. "Stop annoying me child," rasped one parent. "Go and get lost on the beach," ordered another. Luckily, I was able to get an en suite room on the top floor of a hotel with a rolling wood panelled ceiling; but there was head banging danger around the balcony doors where the overhead was cunningly, deceptively low. After the first, sharp painful impact just above the forehead, I resolved to be more careful, but forgot, and had I stayed for a week, might have contracted a permanent brain damage. Having almost knocked myself unconscious for the last time that night, I slept well after moules and boeuf bourgignon eaten in the cramped hotel restaurant.

We pedalled off in the morning on the piste cyclable and shared this for a few kilometres with a young German group – six adults, and two children, riding pillion. Attached to one of their bicycles and in tow, was a trailer contraption on two wheels over-flowing with gear. They told me, as we cycled peacefully through the carless, wooded countryside, that Germans when holidaying abroad try hard to ignore the existence of their fellow citizens when paths cross.

The leader of the pack decided that it was time for a

brew up and I was invited to a mug. We parked off piste, and soon the primus stove brought the water to boiling bubbles in the saucepan as we relaxed on the ground. Thoughtfully, they spoke to each other and to me in English. My host said, "Ah, the water now is cooking. Soon it will be cooked." Tea and coffee were served in stainless steel mugs with tinned milk. It was a good moment, and my roll up tasted especially satisfying. Fritz, in charge of the party, was a keen motorcyclist. He told me about a near fatal accident in which he had been involved a few weeks earlier. It was, naturally, caused by a car he explained scathingly: but due to his reflexes and intuitive reaction, he was able "to crash quite well" and without injury. He asked if we wanted more hot drink. Heads nodded, and he said that he would "cook some more water."

We went on our different ways after this chance meeting and welcome refreshment: they to Bordeaux for the train back to Germany — we to Cap Ferret for the small ferry to Arcachon which I hoped to reach that evening.

The going most of the time on these narrow, mainly level, piste cyclables was fast and thrilling. Occasionally the runway width was reduced to about a foot. The riding had to be done on ill joined, long concrete blocks. Safe when straight, but alarming around corners. Once we came mortifyingly close to a front wheel collision at speed, but swerved just in time. Here and there the piste ran out, and it was main road travel until the shy cycle signs appeared again.

We were between pistes, and on a 'B' type road, when I saw ahead of me, and going in the same direction (they were walking in the middle of the thoroughfare, and in line abreast) two couples wearing nothing but sandals. A camera was slung around the neck of one of the men. There was a naturist resort sign on the left. On seeing this, I supposed that the road we were on was part of the private grounds, and that we were therefore trespassing. Not at all. This was an open highway with appropriate signs and vehicle flow. Traffic of all kinds and nationalities slowed down and passed. No one raised an eyebrow or a hair. Not a single horn hooted. The walkers were middle-aged, portly, and deeply tanned. Their fatness was evenly browned all over. As we approached them for overtake, I coughed — having neither whistle nor bell — and they called out greetings. The glistening, well fleshed, oiled, half inflated buttocks shimmered and danced in the sunlight, rising and falling, quivering and shaking gently like dark brown rugger balls in aspic. I returned their salute, complimenting them on their colour and condition. "Thank you," one of the ladies replied, "brown fat always looks better than white." The five of us, all English, roared, and my own amused fat shook itself about. Then I met and chatted with a couple from Aquitaine who were riding to swim and sunbathe on a nearby beach where, they told me, costume was prohibited, and anyone caught with their trousers up would be harassed by officialdom.

Chapter Nine

Soon we were back on the piste again, but the surface on this section was bad, and the gaps between the thin concrete lengths had become frighteningly wide. I was nervous about the jolting and jarring, and anxious about the hammering that vélo must have been taking. Knowing that its frame was guaranteed for fifteen years was no reassurance. Pausing at a carrefour I remarked on the terrible conditions to a Dutch couple who were also resting. "This is your own bicycle?" the man asked. "Yes? If that were mine, I wouldn't use it on this piste. Ours are rented." This explained the abandoned, unconcerned riding that I had seen all day. We went on, more slowly and watchfully. Before too long, the going was safer and easier.

It was six pm when we arrived at Cap Ferret and I wheeled vélo to the end of the long, confined, ferry pier. I bought a ticket (about four pounds) and Monsieur, officious and angry, told me to remove all baggage from the vélo, pointing, as he did so, to almost perpendicular steps and a small boat bobbing corkily at the bottom of them. I wanted to avoid unfastening all four panniers, the sleeping-bag and bivouac: I got out of his sight, and harm's way, until it was time to board.

The irascible piermaster (he was soon to be even angrier) had been right. When he had given me the order in such an imperious manner I thought that he had been pulling rank — chucking weight around. I was wrong — his rage was wholly justified. I got by him while he was distracted at the top of the steps. He watched me, as petrified, I tried to control the heavy laden vélo and myself on the steep, slippery steps. Gravity took charge as we slithered and lost height. Desperately I tried to save us without knowing how. All the other passengers were safely aboard, and hundreds of strollers on the pier looked down to watch the show. Vélo, without baggage, is in the heavyweight bicycle division. Loaded, in the Sumo league. The captain of the ferry and the piermaster rebuked me loudly, roundly, and in turn. Some of their remarks, published to a great and growing crowd of enthralled spectators, were strongly actionable and might have resulted in substantial damages — and stern words from a fair-minded Judge.

The ferry was already late, as the pier and vessel commanders had announced repeatedly. This fou, idiot, espèce, imbécile, was delaying it even more. We stood at the brink of death, and would die as figures of hate. With every passing second, their contumely hit harder. They addressed the crowds, entreating them to believe that I really was all the things they had in mind, and that would have been at the heart of an interesting defamation trial. In dubio pro populo. When in doubt go to the people. My attackers went to the people — and the people ruled. They were impartial. They knew a free 'end of pier' show when they saw one.

Meanwhile, I was calcified to the vélo, white knuckled hands on both brake controls. We went down one more step without falling into the sea. I heard something behind me — it was the sound of a late, trouble free arrival — a bearded, bespectacled young man coming down the steps two at a time, carrying, in one hand, an empty racing bicycle over his head, which he then passed like a postcard to the captain. Now there was more vituperation. The top and bottom power mad brasses pointed to this paragon, wounding me by comparison. There was a swell of protest in the crowd, who, properly, regarded this as a low blow. I took another step keeping the vélo upright — using it as a crutch. Another — and one more still. The captain then redeemed himself through sheer heroism and strength. His right arm and right leg were aboard the vessel. His left arm and left leg were on the steps, and free. With only centimetres of reach remaining for the heavy snatch and grab, he seized vélo's crossbar, and it was aboard. I congratulated him, and offered a grateful hand. He took it slowly, and with distaste. Reluctantly, he returned the shake, and then looked at my hand in the manner of a person who had picked up something that he would have preferred to throw away. The spectators clapped, and I took the captain's bow for him with thumbs up, V signs, and waves. As we left the pier, I gave them a standing ovation. I took the little remaining bench space in the full cabin, and knew that every eye would be upon me for the half hour plus voyage to Arcachon.

I took out the pouch and lighter and trembling, rolled a bad one. Then an arm went up and it pointed to the 'No smoking' sign. Frustrated, and showing off with a loud sigh, I slowly pocketed the forbidden comforts, and looked astern where the piermaster was still addressing the people, but they were leaving. The people know when the show is over. They know when the curtain falls. On board though, they knew it would rise again soon: in about forty minutes. What would happen (and I could hear them wondering) when I tried to get vélo up the even steeper steps at Arcachon? I had been told this by a bloodthirsty looking man sitting opposite me who angled his hand almost vertically with a dozen 'O la las'.

When we tied up there my shipmates disembarked, rushing up the steps to get the best observation positions for the second and perhaps, even more, dramatic act. The racing cyclist took his vélo, and carrying it in one hand, bounded up the steps two and three at a time. Leaving his on the pier, he rushed down to help me with mine. What a good place the world is, I mused, with people like this racer in it. The captain preferred not to look at me as he and the young expert off-loaded vélo and put it on the steps. I pressed money on him, which he palmed, with his head turned ninety degrees away from mine. The bearded cyclist now took charge, and said he would lift vélo by the front wheel, ordering me to do the same at the rear. This teamwork was good and we reached the top without giving the fans their money's worth. My right hand was between spokes and around the wheel. The bicycle went forward − taking a thin slice of hand skin with it. The bleeding started, and my young life-saver said that he was 'désolée'. I went down to

92

the sea, and put the oozing hand in it, and the water spread red. My fellow passengers were still watching as I covered the pared flesh with a plastic bag which I found on the bottom step: I did this to spare the squeamish, and to let the bag collect the dripping blood. Taking leave of the benevolent cyclist, I wheeled vélo inland and to the broad boulevard behind the beach, looking for iodine and bandages. The watchers went on their ways. They had not seen a drowning but they had been treated to a show of blood, and were unlikely to ask for their money back.

A block behind the broad sea front, we came to a grand hotel. It looked properly snooty. Its forecourt was full of expensive gleaming motor cars. I parked vélo alongside a Porsche or two, observed by a man in the hotel's empty, spacious lobby. Expecting to be given the mother of all bum's rushes in my dirty, bloody, state, I nevertheless walked in, and taking the filthy plastic bag off, showed him my hand — still catching the drops — and smiled. He seemed impressed that I wanted to save the immaculate marble floor from staining, and presumed that I was looking for a chambre, which he assured me he could provide. Then he led me to a tap, and after I had let the cool water run over the thinly filleted, hurting flesh for a few minutes, he returned with ointment and plaster, which he applied, expertly, to the wound. Here was an excellent, nay, exemplary, hotelier. One certainly unmoved by first impressions. An ARGE. An all round good egg. Not an ARBE.

He was a stocky, middle-aged fellow with rimless glasses, and close cropped hair. After treatment, he took vélo and me to a large laundry room with a highly polished floor where there was plenty of space for my Rosinante to rest in luxurious safety. This host's general form elated me, especially when he told me that, in his medical opinion, the hand injury was essentially superficial.

Quixote also had an opulent lodging — en suite facilities with a capacious bath, deep carpeting and double windows opening onto a balcony with wide views of the town. Had it ever been occupied by a cycling tramp before, with two plastic carrier bags for luggage?

For the first time, on arriving somewhere, I had a social

93

plan. From a work experience visit by a Parisienne student to the radio station in Plymouth, I had an invitation from her cousin who lived with parents some twelve miles east of Arcachon. I had met this girl briefly when, she too, visited Plymouth at the same time. I called her on the room telephone. She was surprised, after a bit of helpful prompting, that I had done so well on the vélo. In Plymouth, she was horror-struck when I told her the objective in mind. On this hot summer night in 1991, she was not expecting to hear from me, and I had to coax her gently to recall our one, short, meeting. Only vaguely could she remember the brief encounter and had it not been for the Roscoff/Santander reminder I think she would have regarded me as a 'nutter' trying something different on the 'phone. Indulgently, she said that she and a friend would arrive at the hotel in an hour.

This gave me time for a rare frolic in the bathtub, and when they walked in punctually at nine pm, I was close to some longed for, overdue, feelings of euphoria. Now I was in a car with two attractive young women (the cousin blonde, her friend, brunette) being driven through the elegant, and I daresay, fashionable, Arcachon to see the Grande dune de Pyla some twelve kilometres away. This is the highest beach sand mountain in France (I have heard in the world) stretching south for many miles: In its way, this gigantic golden mass was as spectacular a sight for me as Niagara Falls had been when I saw that wonder first.

At about ten forty-five pm, we settled at a verandah table in a restaurant in an older part of the town. It was not crowded, and the staff were pleased to see us — the head waiter especially so. He helped us to feel suitably en fête. We drank copiously and ate richly. By the end of our carousing and feasting at this place, we had become a foursome. At closing time, the serveur, brimming with local knowledge and contacts, took us to several other establishments. Liberally in liquor, I formed the impression that one or two of these might have been on the moderately disreputable side, but I cannot be sure. Nor can I give a reliable description or account, because I have no recollection of returning to the hotel. I do know, however, that I called for repeated reassurances that I was not being a painful bicycle bore as I told my tale. A final memory was of an invitation to dinner the following evening. My next bout of consciousness was sickeningly miserable. I woke up, fully dressed, and saw that it was eleven thirty in the morning. I was suffering acutely in all ways from the night's unexpected revelry.

When fully awake, I was aware that I had disgraced myself on the floor at the side of the wide double bed. My wife, who had bravely witnessed this disgusting experience once or twice before, in a not altogether idyllic life, would have known what to do ahead of the actual moments of the repugnant, critical, eruption. She would have placed, with careful accuracy, a large bucket at bedside, thus avoiding the repulsive task that I now, in deep remorse, faced. But she was not there. I was alone in these sumptuous quarters, and would have to cope — and I wished that life would end. I staggered to the balcony, having opened the double windows wide, and let in hot, relatively fresh air hoping that it might reduce the bilious stomach acid stench which by now had become unbearably revolting. Putting my hands on the fairly low balcony wall, I looked down — for a second.

I filled the bath and then worked for an hour with towels and soap hoping that the desecrated, abdomen spoiled air in the room had not gone beyond the door, and that the warm breeze from outside, and heat of the day, would soon dry the carpet, and that no one would discover the shameful thing that I had done.

As I was wishing for all this, there was a knock on the door and I heard the turn of a key. A guardian angel, not I, had bolted it. Without moving, and with voice raised I asked the chambermaid for a few more minutes. This was granted, but my checkout deadline was near as I had booked in for one night only. I spoke to the good samaritan in reception on the 'phone, and he said that I could certainly stay another day. The execrable news had obviously not reached him, but was it known to the domestic, whose nostrils, during our fleeting exchange, must have been dangerously close to the keyhole? I never did find out, and continued to be treated with much courtesy. I coveted a can of air freshener, and would have polluted the whole floor with its contents.

I walked, walked and walked again, trying to sweat out all

the toxic poisons carelessly drunk the night before, and by evening had more or less restored myself to normal. Not knowing about the arrangements for dinner on my second night in Arcachon, when I would be the guest, I thought it best to stay in the hotel and wait for a 'phone call. This came from the cousin at nine thirty pm, with the announcement that they would pick me up at ten for dinner at her parents' home about fifteen kilometres from the centre of Arcachon. Maman and Papa were in northern France at the time preparing for a family wedding which their daughter would attend in due course. As I waited for them in the hotel lobby over a restoring beer, I resolved to be more moderate in food and drink this night. At the same time, and with undeserved relief, I realised that while I had befouled the carpet in my room at dawn that morning, the sheets, miraculously, were missed.

At ten thirty we arrived at the cousin's pleasant one storey house with a large garden. We took our places at a longish dining-table, but the family dog was not pleased that I was invited to take Papa's chair.

Aperitifs, nuts, and other nutritious oddments lay in wait and soon my glass was tinkling merrily as ice joined Scotch. The girls asked about my day, and I asked about theirs. They had not much to report — a little tiredness had taxed them slightly more than usual in the pharmacy where they worked — but that was all. They appeared to have taken the previous night's rigours easily in their stride. I told them about my long walk, and my visit to a luxury hotel. I was drawn to this by a large hoarding and picture of an inviting swimming-pool. In the oppressive reception area, Madame — blonde and with much lipstick — said in answer to my enquiry as to whether non-residents could swim for a consideration, "Non, Monsieur," and sent me packing. Her 'Non' was loud and definitive. She enjoyed the word. It may have been her favourite. The lady reminded me of Madame in the bank at Soulac-sur-Mer. I left with what I hoped was a suitable hauteur, questioning as to whether I had given her similar pleasure. At the revolving door I turned for a final look. She was flushing a bit.

Cousin said that our waiter (by now I was less sure of his

rank) had fallen in love with them both, and that he would be joining us, not for dinner, but for digestifs at about one in the morning, when his work was done.

The happy hour was convivially prolonged. At a quarter to midnight we started to have ice cold local oyster, filet steak and frites, cheeses, coffee and cognac. We were a good threesome, talking light-heartedly well. At half past one, the waiter arrived with his colleague the chef, who was not expected. We were now five, and left for another round of visits to various bars. This time it was five thirty when the hotel bed and I met each other again, and while there was neither nausea nor memory loss, I did experience something which I had never known before.

Oblivion came at once. When I next woke up, however, I was standing on the floor below my room. There had been no dream, and so far as I know I had never done any sleep-walking before. My mind and faculties all seemed normal as I tried to work out whether I was a floor too high, or too low. Guessing, I took the stairs up one flight, and went through the room's open door. This phenomenon startled and disturbed me. During my somnambulism, I had risen from the bed, and must have performed complicated functions such as unfastening the door locks, and finding the stairway — or I may have used the lift for descent. By whichever means, I shall never know how I travelled. My subconscious took me down. At that early hour, I must have been unobserved. I gave thanks, because in the hot, balmy air, I had removed all clothing and had retired wearing wristwatch only. It was seven fifteen am. The portion of my brain controlling the sleepwalk must have decided that costume was unnecessary for this dawn patrol. Returning to bed, I wrapped a towel around my waist as a just in case precaution, and wondered if it was safe to sleep again. It was, and on waking at ten thirty, I felt well enough to continue riding south.

Paying the bill (Access this time) to which I added a generous percentage, I took cordial leave of the friendliest possible, and I suspect, most discreet, reception manager. I had arrived dripping blood, had been bodily dirty, and sweatily unpleasant. I may have left a permanently damaged room carpet: I would have provoked serious shock, even

97

e

heart attack, if staff or other guests had seen me sleep-walking: but I detected not the slightest sign of displeasure as he waved and watched us wobble off his beautifully kept, flowered, forecourt.

What was wrong with vélo's rear this time? I thought it better to give Arcachon a swift pair of wheels before Bacchus and Lucullus could get hold of me again and accordingly did not try to find bicycle repair man in the town.

Chapter Ten

The road let me see again the Great Dune of Pyla — massive in its quantity of driven, sea thrown sand. The highway was full of fast traffic, and we had to be careful in the saddle. Soon we met more rolling hills; I tired and decided on an early check in at a tent renting campsite — if we could find one. We stopped at a picturesque wooded spot by the sea where many people were suspended in the air several hundred feet above ground as if by parachute — but they were not coming down. Baffled, I assumed there was a kind of 'stay up for as long as you can' competition, and looked and listened for aeroplanes. I asked about it at the reception desk of the campsite, and was told by the friendly people there that I had been watching the sport of paraponting. One just jumps off the top of a high dune, and the rest is left to air currents, and one's own skill, harnessed to a rectangular parasol over-head.

Determining not to start lessons that afternoon, or ever, I enquired about tentage rental on their large, many acred site. The owner's son was a keen cyclist, honestly interested in my story to date, and he diagnosed bearing trouble as the cause of our rear wheel wobble. This sounded ominous. While understanding nothing about a bearing's work, I appreciated that this particular and crucial item had a starring role to play in the working of machinery. Did not boffins during World War Two say that if we could get the Germans by the ball bearings in their Ruhr factories, Hitler's heart and mind would soon follow? I did not like what this young campsite operator had told me, and now regarded a cycle service garage visit as the highest of all our priorities.

He took me to a wall map, and pointing to a number, said that I could stay there in a tent. I found the pitch, after taking a few wrong turnings, and discovered a tent caravan rig like the one I had occupied, and often surrendered to the teenagers, near St. Jean de Monts. I unzipped the front door, but the caravan itself was locked: However, as the empty tent compartment was all that I required, I stayed calm. This tent space on its own was enough — a shelter where I could lie in bag and bivouac on the sandy ground: There was plenty of room inside for vélo as well. Always I worried about the safety and condition of the bicycle. Its well being had become as vital to me as that of his camel to the Bedouin on a desert journey. I zipped up, closed the tent, and set out for the beach, a long steep way down the dune's cliff. The only passage was by way of a terrifying, precipitous, sand slippery staircase which swayed with every step. Vertigo sufferers should not attempt this. I looked for warning signs, but saw none.

After a few quiet hours watching the paraponters watching us, I climbed up the sand mountain, hanging on to the loose ropes at the sides of the stairs, and went back to my tent home, thinking, drooling, about cold beer followed by something to eat. I saw vélo — outside the tent and on its stand. A dreadful mix-up had been caused by my poor French. What the management really meant, I now embarrassingly found out, was that I should have had a rendezvous at that particular tent with a man on a motor-cycle. He would then have piloted me to an empty pitch where I could erect one of their rig-it-yourself tents. My unsound French had failed me, and I felt undone. I apologised to all concerned, especially to the lawful occupant who had arrived while I was at the beach. He had made his booking the year before. The family were charming to me: bicycles were fastened to the roof of their large estate car.

At this campsite, visitors were required to leave passports and a deposit. I retrieved both: the office, though shut, was unhesitatingly opened when I said that it would be better if I left for a hotel. I had passed one upon a hill, set a fair bit off the road. Going back a couple of kilometres I came to it — a strange, apparently unoccupied place. There was no

one about — in high August. I whistled, hummed and sang a
line or two from *Je Regrette Rien* but there was no response
in these weird premises. I stepped noisily into the eeriness,
fetching up in a salon with pot plants, paintings, tapestries,
antique furniture and a grand piano in one corner.

Sitting on chaise-longues were two silent ladies, totally
indifferent to my arrival. Hoping that they had something
officially to do with the building, and were not grieving
guests, I asked if I might have a room. The more senior
lady said, almost in a whisper, that there was just one
chambre left at four hundred francs — in nineteen ninety-
one, about forty pounds. This was much more than I had
ever paid on the ride for a night's lodging; but I was fatigued,
fretful, and thought that I may as well face the rip-off,
hoping that we could do our business with plastic. Shaking
their heads sideways and in unison, they said together, as if
in verse choir, "No cards of any kind. Certainly not. No
cards. Cash, travellers' cheques, or Eurocheques. That's
all. Nothing else. No cards."

I had four hundred and twelve francs on me. If I stayed
here, there would be another cash flow crisis in the morning.
I was mentally and bodily weary, agitated, and smarting
from the reprimand that I had just received which made
me feel spiritually unclean. Plastic money cards here were
clearly more accursed than blue movies in Frinton-on-Sea.

I scolded myself yet again and rued the time, it seemed so
long ago, when I decided to start on this foolishness: this
downright folly. Also, I was hungry and even if this gloomy
dump served food, I could not have afforded it. In the
shadows, and off the creepy room, I saw what looked like
a bar. It was unlit, dishcloths were spread over the controls —
but in the lifeless area I did see packets of crisps and peanuts.
I had just enough money for some of both, and borrowing
a saucer, made a mélange of these. In the panniers were two
large, hot bottles of La Grande Blonde beer by Monsieur
Kanterbrau which I had purchased from a supermarket earlier
in the day. There was, as part of this overpriced accommodation, a balcony with a rickety table and chair, and it was
there that I made a dinner of potato crisps and nuts, sent
down with two litres of unpleasantly warm beer. In the sultry

heat of the night, I was mesmerised by the lights of dense holiday traffic on the perilous, winding road below. I meditated on the people in these vehicles. Had they had, or were they going to have good holidays? Were they pleased, or not, with the world and their part in it?

I slept relatively well, leaving the balcony windows wide open, and was lulled by the perpetual rhythmic rushes of the impatiently accelerated engines. At least, I told myself selfishly, I did not have to worry about broken fan belts, and boiling radiators, only a wobblier and wobblier back wheel. Did they, in any case, still make cars with fan belts and radiators that could boil over?

In the morning I paid the younger of the two solemn ladies four hundred francs which left me with only a few rattling centimes. I could not afford le petit déjeuner, goaded as I was by the aroma of coffee, and the sight of croissants.

Vélo had spent the night in a garage. I was relieved that its billet had not been added to the account. As soon as we got underway again, I could feel the wheel wobble worsening, with every revolution. So bad was it, that I seriously considered getting off and walking. The going at the time was fairly flat, but I reduced speed, ready for disaster at any moment. We stopped at the first motor garage we came to on the same side of the road, and once more I did a circuit and slalom around forecourt pumps asking Madame to observe me and to report on what she could see of the rear wheel alignment. I watched her face as she moved in line astern, and although her expression was grave when I returned to her for hope, she confirmed her predecessor's diagnosis, a hundred or so kilometres behind. Yes, there was a problem but it was petit, très petit. Minuscule. I thanked her, sighed, and we went on to Biscarosse, a site of much military material of the nuclear kind, and as we rolled along in the morning sunshine on the flat road a column of people appeared on the near horizon. They were nuclear protesters carrying banners. At their head a no doubt sincerely committed man strode with a most violent expression holding before him a placard pledging the words 'NON VIOLENT' in huge lettering. We passed by and were given leaflets.

Soon we were in Brighton country, and in the afternoon, having closely followed the coast all the way, we arrived and parked in a chokingly crowded seaside resort where at the reception desk of a Metropole-type hotel, I was offered space in the annex — a confusing walk away. Decisions on where to stay were now based on two criteria. Did they take Visa? Did they take Access? Ruled out were all campsites and chambre d'hôtes — B and B. This hotel was, thankfully, a plastic place; a suitable refuge because I could eat, sleep and pay my debts at a single stroke of the ball-point. That was all that mattered. In my situation, price and quality were irrelevant. I could not seek value for money. In cash terms, I was too poor. Shortage of money hung over me like a dark cloud — even though I had recently been asking the machines (never tilting at those windmills alone) for the maximum number of francs, equivalent to two hundred pounds. In France, bar beer is expensive, and our frequent, mandatory hydration stops cost a lot.

After an expensive dinner on the top tower block floor, I walked along the sea front and was made nervous by the discordant funfairs, and the screaming of the people as they rode, shot, pushed noise making buttons, and were merry with candy floss and hot dogs.

I went back to the annex room on the ground floor and leant through the open window, looking out on dirty sand and hearing the late night dissonance. I closed the window to test the acoustic. Little of the cacophony was shut out, so I chose the cool fresh air, and wished for sleep. It did not come. When at about two in the morning the funfairs were switched off, I realised that the rowdiest revellers were staying in this annex. The impossible racket, in what was an echo chamber of a dwelling complex, went on without cease — but without the dimension of any entertainment. There was no fun of the kind that I had been forced to enjoy in the La Rochelle flea-pit billeted next to the Legionnaire, from whose acts of martiality I was laid low by laughing fever.

At five o'clock I gave up, got up, and sat on the hotel steps waiting for the day to start. At seven thirty, after coffee and croissants, we set off for an inland town that

we had passed through the previous day some nine kilometres away. I longed to find a cycle shop, and a plastic
friendly bank. We came upon a miracle. On approaching
the built-up area, I saw both. Bank and bicycle repairman
Peugeot were close to each other, and on the handily correct
side of the road. There was a hole in the wall at the bank,
and I could see that Monsieur Peugeot was open and ready
for business — albeit dressed in city wear. I was the happiest
human being. No one could have been more joyeux. This
earth was a favoured place, and life on it, precious. Also, and
now I could hardly believe my luck, a helpful man was
already at the money machine, glad to assist. He super-
vised my button pushing, and looked away, as everyone
did, when we came to the secret moments of the service.

We walked along to the cycle shop entrance. In funds
again, and with spirits Heaviside layer high, I approached
with a warm and jovial greeting. I told Monsieur that I
hoped his day would be a good and happy one. Inviting
him to watch, I did a few circuits for his inspection, and
came to rest outside the door. He observed, but said nothing.
He may have belonged to a silent order. Then, languidly,
he pointed to the right-hand side of the rear wheel. He had
seen a long, bulging tear in the fat, wide rubber tyre. How
had I missed it? How had the other experts not seen it when I
had consulted them? Two motor garage forecourt Mesdames,
and the serious young cyclist at the campsite had not spotted
the great rupture. The ladies had declared that the problem
was small, and the young man had diagnosed bearing trouble.
I was mildly out of humour that these three specialists had
let me down; but then I suspected that spotting the cause of
all the anxiety I had suffered might not be so easy, and that
it takes a special talent and wisdom (as only bicycle repair
man can have) to get to the heart of truly bothersome
things. How many more revolutions were left before the
second, the possibly fatal, blow-out occurred, and perhaps
at thirty-five kilometres per hour? I told Monsieur of this
fear but he stood still, arms firmly folded in front of him
like a strike leader at the gate. He looked at me disapprovingly
as I suggested that maybe it was time for a new chambre
(inner tube) and a new pneu (outer tyre) which I could

conveniently pay for. I had already seen the proper plastic money signs.

Monsieur Peugeot spoke for the first time. He reminded me that it was Monday, and as with banks, many other businesses in France were either closed completely, or offered only partial service — and here, it was the mechanics' day off. That was the position, he explained. On Mondays he was open for sales — but not for service. "Come back tomorrow morning," he said, "and the work will be done."

Briefly, I told him my story to date, and with growing urgency I explained the importance of keeping to an impossibly tight schedule culminating in Santander for the ferry that would carry us back in time for me to meet my commitments on the radio.

"Le radio?"

"Oui Monsieur, le radio. Le BBC."

"Le BBC?"

"Oui Monsieur, le BBC, le BBC."

Feeling a bit ashamed (it was the first time that I had offered this conceit to anyone) I nevertheless exploited the moment, and going to a window-ledge, put my arms upon it, and buried my head. I even considered trying a stifled sob or two, but opted against this: he might have questioned whether I was weeping on account of my métier — or the near disabled vélo.

I looked up to see if this bit of stage business was having any effect, but he was not there. He had gone away, noiselessly, so that I could not use the next gambit I had in mind which was to tell him that if I had to wait here for twenty-four hours, I would be forfeiting the precious one day in reserve that I had built into the time and distance calculations. I was even going to risk the extravagance of saying that the data had been verified by not one, but three, different computers. He was obviously fed up with me and had taken his leave without a word. I could not, and did not, blame him. I knew that I had no choice. I would walk vélo into the town, find somewhere to stay and spend a wretchedly unhappy day waiting for Tuesday. At least, I had some cash again.

We were about to move off, when he came out of the shop

105

wearing overalls and carrying keys – keys to the operating theatre at the side. In disbelief, I pinched myself when he told me to take all the baggage off, and bring the vélo to him – masked, gowned, gloved and ready to save us both. My gratitude was ineffable as he suspended vélo in mid-air on the special hanging apparatus, and went to work. I tried, by looks and words, to let him know that, if I could influence Canonisation, I would pull every string in sight so that he could join the Communion of Saints – and by queue jumping if necessary.

Then I saw, but yards away, a hotel, where people on its terrace were having petit déjeuner. My joy was radiating all over the neighbourhood, and I asked Monsieur if there was time for me to go for coffee, and to bring back for him whatever he desired. Never had I toadied so much, never had I been nicer to people than I was to the staff at that hotel as I insisted on clearing a table myself, and personally carrying crockery and cutlery to the kitchen. Never was I keener on my membership of the human race.

After three grand cafés au lait avec du lait chaud (coffee with hot milk) I sauntered, even swaggered a bit, back to Monsieur Superman. He had put the vélo outside on its stand which was proudly primping its new rear pneumatics. I asked the paragon of Peugeot, this perfect human being, to add on to the bill fifteen per cent as a gratuity. He could not understand this, and was no more enlightened after I told him that he had saved my life. He then helped me to replace the baggage on vélo, probably to expedite my departure. Understandably, I think he wanted to see the back of us, and our back wheel, as soon as overdone grovelling would allow.

We rode off, and made good time on flat surfaces. I sang 'Tink-a-tank' from *Trial by Jury* repeatedly, not being able to unstick the needle. For some unfathomable reason I could not get this tune out of my head. We arrived at St. Julien on the côte d'Argent in the region of the Landes with the sun high at noon and had a leisurely hydration stop on the terrace of a leaf-shaded bar where complimentary peanuts and olives in large quantities were served with the ice cold beer. It was an agreeable and relaxing pause. Surprisingly, few people were there and there was little, if any, noise. Monsieur le Patron thought that I would like Plage Coulis which he strongly recommended. Having told him how much I was enjoying the restful tranquillity of his premises, I was surprised and disappointed, subsequently, to arrive in Babel-on-Sea. We left quickly, having first been advised by a market stall holder that a certain piste cyclable would take us all the way to Biarritz — a place I wanted to avoid at all costs, and would miss, I hoped, by taking a road well inland of it.

I found the suggested piste. It was dangerous and full of cyclists getting maximum wear and tear out of their rented mountain bikes. We found the main road again, being careful not to get sucked on to the auto route express.

At about five in the afternoon, after a hot but efficient ride, we arrived at St. Gourgin ready, but not optimistic, for rest and a night's stay. I expected everywhere to be complet and that was so. Parking vélo in the shade of a handy tree, I settled at an outside table of a bar where a German cycling family of four were my neighbours — father, mother and two lean, blond fit looking teenage boys. Many cyclists were here, and their machines, obviously rented, had been carelessly strewn on the ground. Mine stood upright and proud on its stand. I looked at it admiringly. The Germans at the next table were irksomely loud and voluble, and while I had thirst for more beer, I did not like their distracting din. I paid, left, and we went on our way intending to stop next at the first quiet looking spot with beer taps. In any case we had to get to Léon, where Madame at the bar had told me there would be a better chance of finding a room.

After about ten minutes, I was overtaken by the German family whose bierkeller, clamorous voices, had driven me from an otherwise suitable rest stop. For the first time since leaving Roscoff, I felt some anger — not much, but enough to spur and stir me to the chase. We would make a race of it.

Quickly I put vélo into the topmost of our fifteen gears. High adrenalin matched high gear. I overtook the parents. I laughed and shouted to them, "Tour de France, Tour de France. Au secours, au secours." Their smiles, I think, were not heartfelt. I then went for the main competition — their two sons, already out of sight. I knew that even on this perfectly flat road, commentators would say that I still had a mountain to climb. I had it all to do. I just had to power my way ahead, and win this one for England. I could think only of being over moons — and letting ailing parrots see our dust. We would go for it. We would give it our best shot.

Going flat out, and knowing that all this was childish on my part, wrong, unnecessary, and perilously risky, I was nevertheless drunk on the taste of a hunt. In a few minutes I saw them and closed in, shouting without let up "Tour de France, Tour de France. Au secours, au secours." They responded, and in single file gave their vélos full gun, constantly looking over their shoulders at me. With my better gearing, I had more in reserve than they, and my opponents could not increase the distance between us. The road was straight and level. There was no wind. I stayed in their slipstream and waited for a window in the traffic. Gaspingly, I overtook them and kept well ahead for about half a kilometre. Having now 'won', I slowed down, stopped, smirked, and ostentatiously waved them on. Then I tailed them for the rest of the way to Léon with many more "Tour des Frances" and "aux secours."

They turned left at the outskirts of the town — presumably for the campsite nearby. I grinned, waved to them and croaked "aufswiedersen." They replied, but there was no bonhomie in their perfunctory gestures. I glanced back, but of the parents there was no sign. I hoped that my competitive impetuosity had not damaged Anglo-German or Franco-German (for all they knew I was French) relations too much.

This had been a good day for us so far, and I was pleased with vélo and rider. However, I was all in, when spent and tottering, we arrived outside the information bureau in Leon at sevenish and I used the next quarter of an hour reaching for lung air. The office was packed — full of furrow browed, moist, and twitching holiday-makers. I was in no hurry — I had not breath with which to speak on arrival — and so another half hour passed before it was my turn with Madame. I told her that I was 'by vélo', exhausted, and wanted to get my head down somewhere, anywhere. I went outside to smoke, and saw her on the telephone for about twenty minutes. What I had asked for was nigh impossible to procure in that place at that time, but she was good, and tried hard.

Finally she gave me a slip of paper with a name and address written on it. She had also sketched the way to a house where there might be a chambre.

I found the villa easily, and rang the bell at heavy metal double gates at the end of a drive. A dutiful German Shepherd answered, but did not speak. I pushed the bell button several times and waited for ten minutes but no one appeared. The dog turned up from time to time. I went back to the town centre for beer, and an hour later tried again. This time a man arrived at the gate. He was not of the household, but a son-in-law of Madame who, he said positively, would be home within the hour. I decided to return to town, and there to put on a nosebag: I could replace energy, and then make one final attempt to lodge at this good looking residence.

The centre of Léon was thronged, but I found a vacant outside table immediately after a party of six had left it. The table next to me was even larger, and its occupants left a few moments later. They were succeeded by eight of my fellow countrymen and women whose two GB plated cars were parked close by. I ordered some fish and wine. The neighbouring Britons were fairly noisy, and I thought that some of them had to do with media. They moved the table, and came too close to mine. The back of one of their chairs banged against me. There was no apology.

"Let's have a drink here, and then we'll find a shady restaurant somewhere, shall we?" said one man.

"Yes," one of the ladies agreed. "It is a bit, er, niffy here."

Flushing and blushing slightly, I realised that this English woman was probably referring to the olfactory cocktail of French rolling tobacco, sun oil, and sweat coming from me — and the immunity of my own sense of smell. These people soon left, and I was glad. Now, ruffled, I fretted that the waitress would do her work at arm's length — a needless concern. Overworked, she cheerfully cared for us all.

It was nearly eleven when we set out for the third and last assault on the house of the mute German Shepherd. I pressed the familiar bell. This time Madame appeared at once, accompanied by a suddenly raging, snarling, barking German

Shepherd who had made not a sound (had been a barkless guard dog) on my previous two visits. Now, at his pack leader's side, he was piling on the brownie points. She made no move to quieten him; his challenges were so loud that conversation with the chatelaine was impossible. We had to shout across the locked gates. It did not take long. She was complet. Then she brightened, asking me what I intended to do next. Using hands to make a megaphone, I yelled, with a bogus show of confidence, "I shall ride through the night, Madame," and left this match drawn at fifteen all. 'Avoid France in August.' I had heard this often. Good advice. Unheeded.

We returned to the late evening heat of town for a large coffee and small cognac, and to weigh the wisdom of an all night ride. I had not done this before, and questioned how much, or how little, of the road, the portable torch of a headlamp would let me see. Also I felt a bit of disquiet coming on following my Tour de France victory: there was a soupçon of remorse as well. I should not have allowed myself to be annoyed twice this day – once by Germans, once by people from my own country. Long ago, I found a way to deal with smart arse, clever dick, disagreeable, humans. It is merely a matter of reciting thirteen words to oneself. The discovery always works. It has been an infallible master key. Unused today. Thirteen words exactly. They would have saved me from the recklessly stupid road race, and from a flare of bad temper at dinner. But until today, there had been no need to work the magic.

Asking for a final coffee, I realised also that the charm and ritual handshaking, those easy lubricants of life, were hundreds of kilometres behind. That belonged to Brittany and regions more north than this. The more south we went, the more frantically agitated the holidaying desperadoes seemed to be, as were those who served them. I sensed that few people were actually enjoying themselves. On the good selfish side though, I revelled in blissful ignorance of the world, and its muddle and mess. Daily, my dustbin of a head weighed less as I tipped out a year's collection of mental refuse. It was wombing to be a tiny, one person, slow moving universe cocooned against news of events. I drained the coffee cup, spooned out the syrupy sugar, and reflected on the names of a couple of places we had passed through that day. Bias and Carat City. At midnight, I switched on vélo's front and rear lights, and left Léon behind.

Chapter Eleven

When clear of the amber town lighting, I learned that bicycle lights are for being seen and not to see. On the dark, menacing unlit road, with a forest on either side and deep drops by the verges, I knew that I had made a dangerous mistake. I could see a few feet ahead but no more, and only felt slightly safe during the brief intervals between the high beam lights of lividly driven traffic, threatening us from ahead and behind.

After a couple of kilometres, I decided to abandon this suicidal journey and to capitulate with sleeping-bag and bivouac somewhere in the trees off the road — assuming that I could find a crossing over the deep ditches. Then ahead, and on the other side, I saw in bright red neon, the word HOTEL. While I knew that there would be no room, surely, I told myself, they would let me doss down, tramp like, either inside or outside the main building. Lights were on, and there were people at the bar. We were travelling in the direction of Hossegor.

Phewing and cheek blowing in and out, I went through the carefully practised entrance routine to court quick favour. I was 'by vélo' from Roscoff to Santander, suffering great hunger, thirst, and fatigue. I felt that I had won the Tour de France, and if so, was I not more important than Le Président? If I had judged the audiences correctly, this bit of curtain up business usually came off. Tonight, it brought the house down. There was loud laughter and applause — led by Madame la Patronne, kind, matronly and clucking. There must have been some greasepaint in her generous veins, for she came to me from behind the bar, gavel spooned a glass, and called for order. Ringingly, and from good centre stage position, she declaimed her announcement. There was a chambre for Monsieur le Champion, and a safe night in the laundry room for vélo. I led and prolonged the applause for her while she milked the audience, and took several bows. When she confirmed that it was a pleasure to do business with Visa and Access, I called for celebration — and for all present to be happy — on me. Drinks all round. Let us be en fête. All tiredness and bad thoughts drained out of me. I was transformed by the experience, and had the highest opinion of all present. They, and especially Madame, could do no wrong, would never be less than perfect. I was safe and off the road, no longer about to be killed by the screaming night traffic. I felt protected here — well wombed. I flopped upon the large bed, and seconds later the delicious drowsiness came. Oblivion lasted for over nine hours.

On waking, and feeling well slept and refreshed, I noticed and felt many swellings from mosquito bites, but the good anaesthetist, Doctor Knackeredness, had put me out for a long, undisturbed, slumber. After petit déjeuner on the terrace, and some chat with a pleasant motorised couple much interested in what I was doing, who said they envied me greatly, I got out the plastic, signed the paperwork, and said au revoir to Madame with gratitude and not a little sadness. Feeling quite vimmy, we started on the road again bound for what I supposed would be our next overnight staging post, Bayonne.

The weather was unpleasantly hot in the humid overcast, but I was in good spirits, and for the first time, realistically confident that we would reach Santander unaided. Staying in our highest gear for several hours in the new slightly rolling terrain, I gave thought to the Atlantic Pyrenees battle ahead of us, but fast put that out of mind as the car driving reached new levels of aggression. I was frightened on this road nearly all the time. People were not using their motor vehicles for pleasure. This was a race. More, it was a race war. On smoke and water bottle stops, I would try to catch the expressions of these racing drivers. If their facial flashes were reflecting mirrors of their souls, they showed only frustration and belligerence.

These images took me back to my Montreal days, and the

auto route from the city to the Laurentian mountains – a year round resort with skiing in winter, cool lakes and cottages in summer. My mind's eye focused on our cottage at Lac Quatorze Îles (Fourteen Island Lake) and the nerve-wrenching drives on the tolled Laurentian auto route at weekends to wife and children, sometimes stir crazy (Pia at the time did not drive) as they stayed for the summer holiday weeks and I commuted on Friday and Sunday evenings. I remember the alleviated tension of arriving without mishap, whacked out after a troublesome week of work. Happy hour on the verandah, Scandinavian style, with aquavit from the freezer, and cold herring, the two eased down with ice cold beer, preceded by a swim in the lake with the children worn out from their play and the fresh mountain air, almost, but not quite, longing for their beds. Then the barbecue, late at night and the salmon or beef steaks that I had brought from Montreal.

But did I look as I drove then, like the people now driving on this road? Perhaps, but I thought not. A clay tennis court came with our cottage, and as I pedalled, scared, towards Bayonne, I played again the many matches of those hot summer years. They were always against Robert, a French speaking Montreal doctor. We got on well – friends off court: enemies on it. Our matches were intensely competitive. His wife was fair and impartial as a line judge, but his three teenage daughters were fanatically partisan – loyally ruling that Papa was virtually incapable of error. A good man, he frequently over-ruled their decisions. These memories of life in what was once called New France, helped to divert me from the terror of riding a bicycle in this part of the Old.

We arrived at a fork junction, and I could not tell from the map (since Brittany I had navigated from this, the only one I had, featuring the whole of France) whether we should go left or right for Bayonne. Conveniently, between the roads there was a house advertising the sale of wine. I stopped, and asked Madame for guidance. She carried an even larger wooden cosh than the one worn by the retired Air France pilot. She was alert and at the ready, sawing the air with her offensive weapon. It was important to get on with this middle-aged, dark, square built woman. She was accompanied by two children, a boy and girl of 'tween age and a Spaniel type dog. Madame looked at me, and smiled in the confident way of one in control. As I approached her with the map, I was bitten on the right Greenflash tennis shoe by the dog whose strong teeth must have been a source of pride to its dentist. Madame did not rebuke him or her. I was not curious about the gender of this highly conscientious pet. She told me to take the left fork and yes, there was a place to eat and drink, a couple of kilometres up the road.

We found this, and stopped for some hydration; beer and a sandwich. We were evidently in the environs of Anglet, where we would turn inland for Bayonne, it being imperative to avoid Biarritz, to which by now, we were quite close. Here, the traffic was snarled and stationery for long waits. Sitting at an outside table, I could see better the ill-tempered expressions on the faces of most people in these cars, all driving at high speed into traffic jams. We were now nearing, if not already in, Basque country, and I had lost the feel of France. Spanish dishes of all kinds were on menus. There was a change in outlook and manner, a difference as between sweet and dry sherry.

I knew little about the issue of Basque nationalism, and certainly did not want to increase my knowledge of the subject now. But I had learned that the Basques are an ancient people of obscure origin with a unique language and distinctive customs, and that their nationalism is a source of unrest: but I had no reason as a cycling tourist to fear it. As this would be the first time that I had ever been to Spain, I did not know what to expect apart from the Basque claim, when we crossed the frontier at Hendaye, that we would not be in Spain, but in a province of theirs. Politics, territorial disputes, violence. I spat all these confounded headings out of my mind – momentarily annoyed for giving them even the tiniest thought.

There was no convenient way to avoid Bayonne which was the lesser of a two evil option with Biarritz. This town was a centre of sword manufacturing in the sixteenth and seventeenth centuries, and gave its name to the bayonet. We arrived, after increasingly hilly runs, in the late afternoon.

We did not have to go to the town centre though, and so I searched for a sleeping place on the outskirts that would allow us an easy morning exit. After asking for space, any kind, at five hotels, I found a Holiday Inn sort of edifice where there was one en suite room left. I could stay in this, on the strict condition that it would be vacated before eight o'clock the following morning. This was the earliest hotel chuck out time that I had ever known.

I accepted with great pleasure, intending to make an early start, in any case, to clear France the next day. The hotel was close to a busy industrial estate with loud traffic noise. Before happy hour and dinner, both of which habitually, and eagerly, I looked forward to whenever possible, I started a major laundry operation. I had last done this in far away Challans, and I wanted to leave France in a proper condition, or as proper as my limited washing skills and resources would allow. I trusted that there was sufficient lather left in the diminished block of soap (brand name 'Marseilles') that I had bought not far south of Roscoff. I put every single wearable item I had in the bath, including the tennis shoes and flip-flops, and had a high old time in the steaming room with the soap and gallons of hot water. Sweating in the Turkish bath, I pummelled, rubbed and rinsed.

Then I decorated the bedroom with my two polo shirts, one green, one gold; two pairs of drawers, dark blue and well chosen; handkerchiefs four, once white, now grey — badly chosen. Socks, pairs of two — one grey, now near black, one midnight blue originally, but black for some time. Swimming trunks, one, and still more or less green. Trousers, one pair track suit type, near black. Cycling shorts, pairs two, black and denim blue. This done, I then laundered myself in the bath, having removed from it sand, foliage, and a greasy tidemark. After resting moistly for an hour, and looking ahead to the pleasures of the table, I dressed — putting on wet drawers, the still dripping green polo shirt, the water-logged track suit bottoms, and without socks, the tennis shoes which I had again scrubbed with a well doused lavatory brush. When young, I was told repeatedly about the danger of wearing wet clothes. After rain, they had to be taken off immediately, or pneumonia and the end of life would follow.

116

"You'll catch your death . . . " Perforce, I had put this dogma to the test many times since leaving Plymouth, and found it false. Walking around, I circuited the room for several minutes until the actual dripping stopped. Then I strode to the lift on this high floor, bound for the bar and restaurant. I felt well, almost smug, as by contrived sonorous coughing, and loud greetings, I drowned the sound of water music squelching from my feet.

On this occasion, the vélo had de luxe accommodation in a ground floor conference room — exclusive use of the Salon Gorgone and I popped in to see that all was well. It was resting comfortably on its stand by the Chair position. The bar, surprisingly, was empty when I went to it. Presiding was a barman who was either having an off-day, or who had long ago decided that the planet earth was a bloody awful place. Whichever, I understood, and did not tax him. Mournfully, wordlessly, he doled to me the cold ale and complimentary olives which, speaking in a low voice, I had asked for. I took the glass and shallow bowl and walked slowly on the water (in my footwear) to a distant table, leaving my host in peace, or at least, alone.

Dinner, on what I expected to be our last night in France, was disappointingly ordinary, served in a cheerless, uninteresting dining-room. But I was not brought down by this: and even tried to make the waitress laugh. I soon gave up, and sensed a general melancholy in the surroundings. While I was en fête (for no particular reason) all about me people wore grave expressions.

I went to bed early, but had not reckoned on kitchen noise and the smell of burning meat below. Ears and nose were easily assailed through the mandatorily open window in the room. Better sound and stench, than suffocation. But sleep came eventually.

Waking at seven, I packed the humid clothes in their plastic bags, and put all in the panniers, which I then made fast again to the vélo. I had petit déjeuner, paid with Access, and cleared out as agreed by eight o'clock.

Navigating away from Bayonne was confusingly difficult. I could not find an exit, and for an hour and a half took wrong turnings, helplessly lost. Above all, I wanted to avoid entrapment on the auto route express; nevertheless, exasperated, and knowing that we were pedalling into danger, I followed the large signs pointing to St. Jean de Luz and Espagne. I knew that this road would safely bypass Biarritz, and if the worst came to the worst, and I was sucked on to a forbidden motorway, I could stay on the hard shoulder, risk it, and get off at the first exit. Soon we were on one, and there was no turning back. We had passed, again, the point of no return.

In highest gear we made rapid, illegal progress. Once, I thought about stopping and wheeling back to the joining spur, but quickly discarded the idea. We had never moved faster, vélo and I, and but for the gendarmerie, always in mind, I would have enjoyed the sheer speed of it, notwithstanding the hostile horned hooting — belligerent as never before. There was a steady, long blast on this instrument, accompanied by staccato flashing of headlights, from a white transit van on the opposite side of the median barrier. It stopped on its hard shoulder, and so did we on ours. Two men in orange coloured overalls got out, shouting and waving. Weaving, and crossing six lanes of unleashed traffic, they came to us, and I felt unnerved.

As they approached, we were on the outer edge of the hard shoulder still a-saddle, and taking weight on the left leg. I had not seen a drop of three feet to our immediate right and, without thinking, transferred body mass to the other, right, leg. Taking my foot off the right pedal, I put it down without looking — into empty space. We rolled over and fell together, luckily on to grass, our shock absorbed by the soft, fat, bulging panniers. We were shaken, but not wounded, or damaged. I tried to regain dignity and composure after this purler, and to conceal the trembling that had taken hold. I wondered why these men had risked their lives in order to see me.

By now I was sure that they were police of some sort, in boiler suits. It was with relief that I listened to them. They were council highway workers more interested in my welfare and safety, than in rebuking me for law breaking. One of them stayed with me, while the other bravely returned to the vehicle, saying that he would drive off and return on our side so that we could be driven back to a lawful road. We waited several minutes for the rescue. Monsieur and I discussed what the attitude of the gendarmerie would have been, had they met me first. He thought that they would have made lenient allowance, with a severe reprimand. Luckily, I was not obliged to find out.

When the van arrived, we loaded vélo into its cargo area, and I joined Sir Lancelot and Sir Galahad on their front seat bench. I had volunteered to ride with the bicycle, but they were strongly insistent that this would not do. This made me uneasy, a little frightened. I could not now control the situation. Who were these men? Why were they going to all this trouble? What did they want? Until now, the stomach had been calm, and had sent no warning signals. The twitching started when they told me, with such authority, that I must ride with them, and not vélo.

As soon as we drove off, the fear subsided, and the fleeting paranoia fizzled out. In a few minutes, we were off this French motorway and unloading the vélo at a roundabout approach road. My well-wishers pointed to the exit that I should take for St. Jean de Luz. I had already told them how much I wanted to avoid Biarritz, which amused them greatly. "You don't want to go to Biarritz?" one of them asked in phoney horror, "That's really surprising." I liked the way that they had got into the spirit of things, and with matching falsehood, told them that I had been mistaken and was unfairly prejudiced towards the famous resort — watering place of Kings, Queens and Princes. I would go there after all. But not today. Another time, when the traffic might be lighter. Never such a time, they stressed. In that case, what a pity, I said. Our laughter was real.

I gave them repeated thanks, and a one hundred franc note — at the time, slightly more than a tenner. They were amazed, and refused to accept. They took it only after I invited them to have a good déjeuner. They had extricated me from much potential trouble and danger.

It was good, later on, after a stretch of smooth and uneventful running, to see the signs for Biarritz pointing in the opposite direction. We could also have bypassed St. Jean de Luz, but I had a reason to go there.

At school (my parents were in India) I spent a lot of

holiday time, when not with my grandmother in Bournemouth, at the home of a good chum whose father's house was near Salisbury. Father was a prosperous haberdasher who spoke, often and longingly, about a French resort called St. Jean de Luz close to the Spanish frontier. He had divorced his wife, and the son (we shall call him Arthur) was their only child. The marriage was never mentioned, and not once in school days, did Arthur speak of his mother. Father and son did themselves well at home, even in the austere post-war period. The resident housekeeper kept a good table, helped by a full time maid. It was easy to feel part of this household, and Arthur's father could not have been a kinder or more generous host.

As we went down the long hill into St. Jean de Luz, I pictured the clerical grey three piece suited figure with the pipe full of Parson's Pleasure, the thick lenses in the tortoiseshell horn-rimmed frames, the iron grey brushed back hair. Despite his business success and bonhomie, he had, I could now recall, what Pearl S. Buck had once described to me in a Montreal television interview as 'an inner stillness', referring to an American President she had known well. Kennedy. As a schoolboy, I would not have understood that, but would have known something of sadness and of wistfulness. It was this that I always thought Arthur's father felt whenever he spoke about the place we were now approaching. Although that sentiment got through to me as an adolescent, its cause and background would not have mattered. Now, I guessed that he had either met Arthur's mother here, or another. Nostalgic, I wanted to get a taste of the place that he had loved so much.

Parking the vélo at an outside table in a small, leafy square, I went to a bar for café cognac, and watched the elegant world go by. I toasted the memory of those happy school holidays in Wiltshire. Then we climbed the hill, and were quickly on the corniches to the frontier town of Hendaye, and the Atlantic Pyrenees.

On seeing the beach, I recalled that Churchill bathed and painted here on his first post war holiday taken in July 1945, and spent in Hendaye at the château of Bordaberry as the guest of Général Brutinel. When he and party left the sands at the end of their stay, one of his people (Jock Colville) tried five times to pay Monsieur for rental of tents and deck-chairs. Five times payment was refused by the beach operator who said that he would take nothing from the man to whom France owed so much.

Lunch, with knives and forks, has not been part of my life for many years — incompatible with a broadcast start at one fifteen pm — but as we rode along the sea front road at Hendaye, I saw that the time was a quarter past one. Impulsively, I decided to have a celebration middle day feast on the French side of the frontier. We were a two minute ride from Spain, and I wanted to mark our achievement so far, in a suitably French way. Needing to find a restaurant with the right ambience, and one doing business with plastic, I took my time, and rejected several before finding, in a cul de sac with mountain views, the ideal spot.

Madame was sympathetic, interested, and generous with olives, served at an aperitif table in a small court with pleasant tree shade. Monsieur, who was also chef (fortunate pairing thus far in my experience) took vélo to a cool, safe spot and beamed with pleasure when I told him the distance run from Roscoff. He proudly showed me his own three bicycles.

The attractive, damask walled dining-room was on the first floor and the quiet digestible background sound and light classical Muzak, very much to my mood taste. It went down well with the smoked salmon, filet mignon, assorted cheeses, champagne, coffee and Remy Martin.

Monsieur and Madame joined in my good humour. Just before leaving, I said that I would not try to finish the remaining fifty kilometres to Santander that day. Monsieur le Chef had just returned to his kitchens, and so missed this. Wide-eyed, Madame looked at me incredulously, her expression a great question mark. I wondered what it was that I had said which apparently had shocked, if not actually caused offence. "Fifty kilometres, Monsieur?" She shook her head vigorously, and called for her husband. "Non, non, NON," she said with growing emphasis. Had I blasphemed? Why this reaction? Monsieur arrived, wiping hands furiously on his apron, and ready, by the look of the fire in his eyes, for a fight. He wanted to know at once the reason for

121

f

Madame's urgent summons. She explained, and had she been able to speak privately, would have raised the question of my sanity. I too, had done this frequently during recent weeks.

Was I, he asked, still at fever pitch, mistaking Santander for San Sebastian? No, I assured him, not San Sebastian — there's no ferry to Plymouth from there. Only Santander. "Map, map," they said. I had not a map showing even an inch of Spain. Le Chef rushed for his, and was breathless as we poured over it on the table. Measuring, we agreed that the distance was close to three hundred kilometres. I was punctured — but only for moments. My euphoria, at having done the length of France, inflated again in seconds; but I knew that it would be prudent to get a map of sorts, giving the matter, however, no serious priority. I had previously, from an atlas, memorised the route — we would have to go through San Sebastian (for an en route social visit) Bilbao, Laredo. The important ploy, always, was to keep the sea to our right. Cheerily, I bade farewell to these, my final, French, convivial hosts.

There was one more thing left to do in France: that was to change remaining French francs into Spanish pesetas. This I was able to do without fuss in the wet air of a steaming bank, metres from the frontier checkpoints.

Arriving there, I looked back at France, saluting it silently, and whistling a bit of the *Marseillaise*. I wanted to follow with a bar or two of my new host country's national anthem but knew not a note of it; and cursed myself for that, together with a total ignorance of its language. I was aware that due to this Spanish handicap, progress and life would be harder in the days and nights to come. My weak French had laughingly seen me through in France, and I would try to use it as a first language in Spain.

Chapter Twelve

Stopping at a frontier control kiosk, I saw heavy traffic speeding both ways across the border without pausing for pass control. This puzzled me, but I did not move on, waiting for the only uniformed official in sight to finish his long 'phone call. After several minutes I became impatient and walked up and down, coughing and trying to get his attention. I looked at the words 'Spain' and 'Espagne' and at the blue and gold starred Euro flag. Obviously, I was not high on this functionary's list of 'most wanted crossers', but eventually I made eye contact with him. Annoyed at this intrusive interference, and like an impatient point duty policeman, he jerked a thumb towards his country.

For the first time in a fairly well travelled life, I was in Spain, and noted the similarity between their road signing and our own. The fingers pointed more definitely in their directions than in France. Around the frontier town of Irun there was much political graffiti — and in aerosoled English, writ large, 'THIS IS NOT SPAIN'.

Hot drizzle started to fall as we set out for San Sebastian and my spirits sank. There were many stops — mainly for looks behind at France, and for a couple of minutes I even thought of turning back. Now the road signs were pointing to Donostia (the Basque word) as well as to San Sebastian. Bi-lingualism as in Wales, Quebec, Ireland and Brittany.

We were riding into an altogether unfamiliar wilderness with few places inviting us to stop for food and drink. While wheeling the vélo up a young mountain after clearing Irun, we passed a road gang on the other side. Ribald and mocking, they shouted and made glass raising, belly patting, gestures, and I was pleased to join in. It was now about three in the afternoon and the drizzle was getting hotter and thicker, but I wanted to reach San Sebastian that day if possible in order to make contact with a couple who like the people in Arcachon, I had met briefly earlier in the year through the same sort of work experience visit.

The land was becoming more and more hilly, and I could see only mountains ahead. The drizzle had now grown to rain, and had it fallen from a shower-head, I would have made an adjustment to 'cooler'. For all that, I sang during the steepening ups and downs on this road, and chose a selection from *My Fair Lady*. We had Spain, we had the rain. We did not have the plain. So I changed the words a bit, dedicating them to vélo. "The chain in Spain strained vainly in the rain."

The traffic was now frenzied with headlights full on, and windscreen wipers arcing at high speed. I was tiring fast, but forced myself on. After thirty gruelling kilometres from the end of France, we saw the approaches to San Sebastian, which from a distance looked big. On the Bay of Biscay, this port, and resort with a big fishing industry, was also a former royal summer residence. Perhaps it was caused by the wet and overcast weather: I was melancholy as we came to the built-up area of the outskirts. The place seemed grey, and frowning with defiant units of mass housing everywhere. Visually, there was no joie of the kind I had left behind. No shop windows with goodies galore. 'Bar', 'Café', 'Restaurant', 'Hotel' signs were so few, and so far between pedal pushes. Alone, cut off, and lost.

That was the mood, as I stopped to check the acquaintances' contact information. I had to reach Avenida Isabella II and was flummoxed. I felt newly disadvantaged. While I would drink the wine of the country, I would not be asking for it in the proper language. As I did not want to give in by speaking English, I was incommunicado. Who would speak French here? What to do? Where to go? Who to ask? Overcast above, downcast below. Soon we were ensnared by more and more battleground roundabouts, and spaghetti junctions. I fussed about fly-overs and Spanish auto route expresses called, I could see from the signs, 'Auto Pistas'. It was

124

imperative that we avoid them.

I decided to keep going straight on — it was as good a guess as turning, and after a few kilometres more, successfully ignoring all 'Auto Pista' signs, we came to a more pleasant part of the town. There were still massive apartment buildings, but of the more 'up market' variety. Compared with the hideous eyesores we had seen before, these buildings were much easier to look at, and they would probably have hall porters or concierges.

This was the case at the block where we stopped. Senor was in his cubicle on the left of the spotless marble entrance hall. I began by asking him, in French, if he spoke French. He was elderly, with a benign round face, but he spoke only Spanish. I showed him my notebook with the address and 'phone number of the people I was trying to find. He knew exactly where they were, giving and writing detailed instructions, and sketching like Picasso, but I took nothing in. It was impossible to concentrate, bogged down as I was, by the painful reality of my lingual inadequacy.

A terrible sneezing came upon me, and excusing myself, I went outside and let the trumpets blast. The spasm spent itself. I had just finished the twelfth and final nasal orgasm (I always count the number of these tax free pleasures) when I heard youthful voices speaking English in American accents. It was a wonderful sound, made by a couple of dark skinned, Phillipino youngsters who, helmeted, pulled up at the entrance on skateboards. They looked about ten years old. Could they, I asked, find out if Senor in his cubby-hole would let me use the 'phone which I had seen on his table? They thought that this was not a good idea. I suspected that he and they were not on the best of terms. Perhaps they had differed in the past on the rights and wrongs of skateboarding on the perfect marble surface inside.

The older looking boy, whose tailor would have known him as a junior client with the fuller figure, took charge. He and his fellow skateboarder were cousins, the other being as puny as he was big. We conferred, outside, about baseball, where I got on with a much needed roll up. Then I went inside to collect the directions and sketches from Senor, who stressed the importance of somewhere called Amara

Nuievo by underlining the words heavily, and waving an arm in all directions. I looked balefully at his telephone, and with as much supplication as I could arrange, tried to make of my face a polite question mark. His head shook violently sideways and I knew that there was nothing doing. I thanked him nevertheless with a smile and a few handclaps, and returned to my new friends outside who, I hoped, would also be helpers. Having told me that his thin cousin lived in New York, and that he was "vacationing right here in our apartment," the senior lad and I got down to business.

"What's your problem?"

"I've arrived in San Sebastian, after riding this bicycle from northern France. From Roscoff in Brittany."

"So?" And away he went with his cousin for a bit more skateboarding.

"So?" I repeated after him.

"Yeah, so what's the big deal?"

"No big deal," I replied. How could, how would these youngsters ever know that this was one of the biggest deals of my life? As casually as I could, I went on. "No, no. No big deal. The problem is that I don't speak Spanish. I'm lost. Trying to find some people in San Sebastian. Moreover, I have not understood a word of the directions given to me by Senor the concierge." This pleased them.

"I got a good idea," young Buntero said. "C'mon, follow me."

He led us, minus skateboard, to the lift area, and pressed an intercom button. A pleasant American female voice answered.

"Hello?"

"Mom? Listen. There's a fat guy down here on a bicycle and he needs help."

Without pause his mother said, "OK. Does that mean I have to come down, or is he coming up here?"

I could not believe this luck. I accepted her invitation, but was anxious about the vélo's security. Mom heard me banging on about this, and cut in with, "You two guys keep an eye on that bicycle, OK?" She gave me lift instructions, and I gave her my first name. Who were these people, I asked myself, while waiting for the lift. There was still

126

trust? The hoist arrived, and the children went out again to their skateboards. I noted the large amount of space in the 'elevator car' and would use the observation for small talk, if necessary. It was not.

Their apartment was on the sixth floor with direct entry from the lift. Mom met me at the door as if I were a relative dropping in for the weekly visit.

"Hi, David. Good to see you. What would you like? Tea? Coffee? Beer? Something stronger? A bit of lunch? We're just finishing. Had to go to the airport this morning to see his brother off to New York after vacation." And she pointed to her husband, a pleasant, fit looking man, who sat at a dining-table in a corner of the large, daylight filled, room.

I felt rescued by this warm, delivering, kindness, but sought nothing more than street directions in English. It was half past four, and after an introduction to the boys' grandmother, who spoke only Spanish, my unpleasant feet were well and truly under the table. I had cold beer with a variety of tasty snacks, the family talk flowing easily. This was surprisingly good fortune. I no longer felt shipwrecked, sheltered by these poised, relaxed Philippinos.

They suggested that I should stay in San Sebastian long enough to meet some of their friends, and enjoy a bit of social life in the English speaking milieu. I had neither appetite nor costume for this, and stressed the pressure of the ferry timetable as a way out. They were the sort of people who would have easily provided the proper state of mind and clothing. They were unusually glad to be alive.

Two hours later, and on their portable 'phone, I spoke to my surprised contacts in Avenida Isabella II and with a well sketched map, we were on our way. The good samaritanos had given me their card. I tried to convey my gratitude for their instant, trusting, goodness. I had asked no questions about their business backgrounds, or lives. Neither had they, about mine. This was a good beginning in Spain. I marvelled as I rode, with paper sketch clenched in teeth, at the way they had received a dirty, mapless, foreign cyclist. Olé. Bueno. It was uplifting to think that what had been done, could be done, in an increasingly mean spirited world. We were in ETA country. Separatism. Montreal and the FLQ. The kidnapping of British Trade Commissioner Jasper Cross. The murder of Quebec's Labour Minister, Pierre Laporte. The world — a difficult place to shake off.

I concentrated on the names of roads and turnings, making a mental note to call Skateboard Mansions if and when I reached my destination safely. I would convey special thanks to that other fat guy, and his cousin, who had called Mom on the intercom again, when they left the grounds, to announce that the concierge now had vélo under surveillance.

We approached the centre of San Sebastian — a bit Venetian with its canal-like river-ways and bridges. I stopped on one of these (with sighs) because in spite of the best possible directions, we were lost again, and in a renewed state of agitato. I asked a passer-by, carrying briefcase, in French, to help me. He had no French, but his English was perfect, and he told me clearly that I was now close to destination, and which turns to take.

Avenida Isabella II is a wide divided boulevard with, on both sides, tall apartment blocks joined together, and commercial premises at street level. Franco in his time, had ordered colossal building programmes — flats for inexpensive occupancy — and while architecturally ascetic eyebrows could be raised at the result, it turned out that their construction (I found out later) was pragmatic, and politically sound. He was determined that homeless people would never threaten him.

We arrived at the main door of such a building, and stuck to it was a note addressed to me — in English. It said that my hosts would be back at seven. It was now just after six, and warm rain had started to fall anew out of the overcast. A few doors away was one of many bars in the thoroughfare. Leaving vélo in sight, I went into a narrow room, its floor ankle deep in tissue paper. This was my first visit to a Spanish pub and to tapas, which I had heard about from others — some of whom had holidayed in no other country. Mouth wateringly delicious in appearance, these snacks covered the counter — constantly replenished with plates of the savoury delicacies. Canapés and hors d'oeuvres had never looked or tasted like these.

They were very moreish, and I assumed that they were free.

I was not aware of any dinner arrangements later on, so tucked in; and conformed to local custom and practice by dropping small bundles of oily tissues on the floor. How generously civilised was the Spanish licensed victualler. This was the way to do it. All these freebies. It makes good sense. People want to drink extra with a bit of salt and savoury inside them. How very much better than peanuts and crisps. I was doing myself so well that I stopped only just short of the 'full' mark, leaving a little space in case there was more eating to come.

With a final gluttonous look at the snacks, I signalled for the bill, and gave the plates of tapas a standing ovation. From beneath his Groucho Marxist moustache, the barman changed his expression from solemn to half grin — and nodded twice. Then he did his sums at the cash register. I looked at the figure on the chitty, and by some coarse mental arithmetic, computed the price of beer in Spanish bars to be more prohibitive even than in France. The peseta dropped. There is no such thing as a free tapas. Groucho's sharp practised eyes had seen my every reach and take.

There was still half an hour to fill before seven, so we walked our way along Avenida Isabella II to another, larger, colonnaded, bar. It was raining heavily and people at a table outside, but under cover, helpfully moved their furniture in the crowded space so that vélo and I could keep dry. I had some more beer, but no tapas, and listened to the babble sound of San Sebastian, the day's work and shopping done. Next to me were four ladies, one of them unable to take her eyes off vélo. As they left, she said good-bye, in Spanish, English, French and German. Knowing this was meant for me, I rose, bowed deeply, and clapped. She and her three companions returned the applause, blew kisses, opened umbrellas and stepped out, chortling in the wet.

A few minutes after seven, we went back to the apartment building. The note had been removed. I pressed my hosts' button and the loudspeaker crackled. "The only way to secure your bicycle is to bring it up in the lift," Miguel said, adding and I was grateful to hear this, "I'll be right down." The electronically controlled doors opened, we exchanged greetings and lifted the heavy, baggage laden, Raleigh Magnum inside, and up to the lift doors.

Miguel took charge. He was a cyclist himself, a serious one, and told me to take all luggage off the vélo. He spoke from much experience. The panniers would travel in one lift with him, while I, by steadying the vélo on its hind quarters would escort it in perpendicular mode up to their home on the ninth floor. I reflected, as I wrestled with the faithful machine, how many fully loaded bicycles could have fitted, with both wheels down, in the lifts at Skateboard Mansions. Here, there was just enough room, with a few centimetres to spare. Vélo was unco-operative. We dead heated with the baggage lift. Anita was waiting, and we settled the bicycle down on a small balcony at the back.

There were two bedrooms, one used more as a store from the look of things. I was invited to stay for as long as I wished. They gave me the choice of foam on the floor in this room, or the convertible sofa arrangement in the living-room which led onto a spacious front balcony overlooking the Avenida. I opted for sleeping-bag on floor foam, thanked them for their generous welcome at no notice, and said that I would like to stay the night, and perhaps a second, but no more. They wanted me to know that they were casual hosts, and gave me keys so that I could come and go as I liked. After a refreshing, awakening shower, we walked to their car a street or so away, with laments over the universal parking problem, and at about nine, drove off for dinner in an old part of the town.

They were well known in the restaurant, and I was deeply contented as we started on the aperitivos. Heedless of where I was, I raised a glass in toast, and proposed "Viva Espagna" — and then began to sing it. This was mindlessly tactless, as Miguel gently pointed out.

"I wouldn't sing that particular song here, if I were you, David," he cautioned.

Anita laughingly added, "He's right, of course, but it's all much foolish. Every politics is foolish."

We all agreed with this, and the fresh toast was "Damnation to all politics."

I asked them to explain, in brief, easy to follow terms,

what all this Basque separatist business was about. Miguel
said that I had asked for the impossible, but that if I wanted
to listen for several hours . . . ? No. It was a congenialiy
festive evening. After dinner, with limitless wine going down
with several different dishes of meat and fish taken and
shared Chinese style between us, we moved to another
swinging locale for champagne. They said that we must
celebrate in fiesta style my arrival in northern Spain (Basque
Province) and my first visit to San Sebastian (Donostia),
Plymouth's twin city. In the restaurant where we had dined,
I had agreed (or so I thought) with the waitress, who looked
like Miss Spain and Miss Basque rolled together, that I should
pay the bill. When the time came, however, she told me that
this had already been done by the adamant Miguel. Now,
at least, I could get my own back with the early hours
champagne. It was well after three when we gave up. I was
concerned that they would be tired at seven thirty — their
time for work with computers in a bank.

In the too hot bag, I sweated heavily, and rested poorly,
with only fitful minutes of sleep. After my hosts had left, I
made several cups of tea which I took out to the balcony.
This apartment, if larger, would havc been called a penthouse.
The view was not exotic, there was no sight of the sea, but
from this altitude, one looked over most other buildings.

I was not sure how to spend the day, even less, the
evening. Hammer blows hurt the head, and hands trembled
when I tried to hold the teacup with its too small handle,
preventing proper finger insertion and through grip. Was it
too soon I wondered, and would it annoy Fate, if I found a
travel agent and made the ferry booking? Aboard the
Bretagne? Or would that be dangerous? No, it would not, I
gambled. Such was my confidence by this time, that I did
not question any more, our unaided ability to reach Santander. Not for me the superstition of sailing ship days, when
it was believed that the cleaning of boots before landfall
would bring grievous luck; but I divined what happened
later as a definite sign, and thought no more of booking
ahead. It took all morning to find anyone in the travel
business, as if one were meant to seek, but not to find.
When I did, the mildly mournful fellow behind the counter

made a 'phone call, and then told me simply to turn up at the ferry terminal in Santander. Nothing more could be done from San Sebastian. That was good enough, and I went to tapas then, and to the reviving company of some hairs of dogs.

I spent the day wandering around, pacing myself from tapas bar to tapas bar, slowly drinking glasses of cold, foamy beer, and trying to work out how, next morning, I would (single handed) reload vélo on the ground floor after it, and the pannier baggage had travelled down in the lift separately — all without Miguel's reliable supervision. Increasingly depressed, I went back and forth to the flat, making cups of tea, worrying about the morning, and departure.

In the evening we were quiet, chatting and eating lightly. All were to sleep better, but before bed — or in any case — bag, I asked if I could make a check-in home 'phone call before leaving. "Certainly," Miguel said. "But this is important. You must not, repeat not, think of leaving any money on the table to pay for it. I shall be offended if you do." We said our good-byes, our adios.

In the morning they must have left soundlessly, or my sleep may have been deep. It was about eight o'clock, and I dezipped myself from the sleeping-bag, swiss rolling it tightly to fit in its now dirty, once bright orange nylon casing. I started on the first of many cups of tea, and then made the 'phone call. All was well, I was pleased and relieved to hear, during the thirty second conversation. A kind of elation usually sets in after these routine calls. Most of the time, in solitude, thoughts are free to roam. Crises, en vélo, requiring concentration come and go. Some thinking is carefree and good, some, unwholesome and bad: so that when one is told cheerfully on the 'phone that there have been no accidents, illnesses, robberies or fires, the psychological charge for a while can be so great that steep hills, otherwise unchallenged even by our lowest gear, are taken on, and beaten.

I thought about the climbs to come — we now faced mountains just about all the way. I still had no map but Miguel had briefed me well. He knew the journey — as cyclist and motorist. He had tried to explain as casually as he could, that at times I would find the going heavy. It would be hard riding. I realised how tough it would be, when he suggested that we had actually accomplished our mission. San Sebastian surely was journey's end. Plymouth, after all, was twinned with it. He said that by doing this, I had performed a great feat. That must be enough. Santander and Plymouth only had a ferry link in common. "You can now go head high some of the way by vélo, some by bus, and some by train. That will also give you a taste of our public transport." I was tempted, but would not fall. My hosts were being sensible. Practical. Logical. Wrong. Santander had always been the objective. Ferry to ferry. Not twin city to twin city. Vélo and I would do this on our own — every metre of the way. But they prepared and braced me for the ordeal in waiting. For the cursing and despair to come.

They had been good hosts, although they would have denied this. All I could do by way of appreciation was to leave a small jar of duck paté that I had bought long ago near St. Jean de Monts. I left a note with 'Thank you' written in Spanish, French and English. Still worried about getting vélo safely packed and on the road again, I put off the work and brewed tea three times more. I looked at Anita's picture on the wall. She had the kind of eyes that people write songs about. After one last tea, I tidied up the kitchen, and the place where I had slept, and got on with the job.

Vélo reared, and played up even more this time. It did not like lift riding, frustrating several attempts to place it upright with the front wheel jammed high in a corner, and with about two inches of space left for door closing. With one foot keeping the door open, I had to deny others their ups and downs. Finally, we were both inside and on our way. Residents at the bottom were not pleased, for it had taken a long time to get this operation right. One or two believed that the whole system had broken down. Sweating, and out of sorts, I looked ingratiatingly at them, and contritely made myself busy. Then I parked the empty vélo by the main entrance, and thought of Sam Goldwyn, and David Niven's book, but with empty bicycles, not horses.

When I returned to the apartment for the baggage, I could

not open the front door. My stomach plunged, and dropped through all nine floors. Now what? Providentially, voices I heard on the level immediately below belonged to Senor the concierge, and Senora. I bounded down the stairs and shaking, showed them the keys and pointed up. Calmly Senor walked with me and opened the door. Het up, I had turned the key the wrong way. I asked him to oversee my last locking of the door once I had put all the baggage outside. After attaching every pannier to the vélo, I could not find Miguel's letter-box. We had agreed that I would leave the keys in there. I could see neither name nor number and was obliged to disturb Senor again by using the intercom button, which I was able to find. He looked at me as if questioning the Creator's wisdom, took the keys, and put them in the correct mail slot.

After following Miguel's general directions for leaving San Sebastian, we were soon lost, but put right by the owner of a tapas bar. We went up an obstinate hill, and met a cycling group coming down. They slowed, and stopped for a spell of map reading. We exchanged greetings in basic body language. No Spanish from me, no French or English from them. They were from Barthalowner, bound for Pamplona.

Chapter Thirteen

When we had cleared San Sebastian, I knew that our high kilometre scoring days were over. Mountains now encircled us. I decided that these were unworthy enemies — we would not fight them to the death. We would not even tilt. Whenever our lowest gear reduced us to walking speed or less, I wheeled vélo until we were ready to ride. Up and down, up and down. When would we see a horizon again? We slowly rose and quickly fell through country which, while beautiful in its rugged way, was also hostile, high, and menacing. It threatened. Unfriendly and not to be messed about with. I missed the pleasure-giving road signs of France. 'Bar', 'Crêperie', 'Café', 'Restaurant', 'Hotel', 'Gites d'étapes', 'Chambres d'hôtes'. Here was a hedonistic wilderness. We were in a rarefied, oasis sparse, desert. Coca cola signs reigned on these roads, while Kronenbourg, Kanterbrau and Jupiler wore their crowns in Gaul.

After a couple of hours of heavy riding, we came to a small, quiet, village on the N634, a road we would stick on as it went all the way to Santander, even though other roads would take us closer to the sea, and perhaps reveal nicer scenery. Still mapless, we stopped in this tiny place where there was a restaurant sign. The door was wide open, and many talkative people were inside, but they were not open for business. The family run establishment was closed — they were on holiday, in high August — in catering. I thought about the custom they must be losing, and how differently their counterparts in other European countries would view things. Then I recognised the irrelevancy of this comparison. The people inside, by the sound of glassware, cutlery and plates, were treating themselves well, without hurry. Under my breath, I proposed a Spanish toast to them, "Salut, y amor, y dinero, y tiempo para gastales." — "Health, Love, Money, and the time to enjoy them."

After a few more kilometric ups and downs, we came to a much snootier place, isolated, off the road, and definitely open for business. This too was family run, and the daughter of the house was keen to speak and improve, her already good English. Although I had not lunched routinely thus far on the ride, I found the mountain air and gravity induced exertion to be appetite sharpening. Besides, stomach was loudly a-rumble. I reckoned that a good feed now would produce therapeutic, as well as alimentary, satisfaction. One wanted to scoff. One required a belly boost.

I was peaceful at an outside terrace table with a red cloth high above the ground where I could see vélo resting below. Otherwise the view was of mountains, mountains, and more mountains — their peaks hidden by hot low lying cloud, giving oppressive, sweat making air. Daughter brought me sopa, steak and wine. Her cheerful, sporadic, company gave me lift.

Sated, we continued our assault course on the N634. I still had no map, but it was a road number that I had memorised in San Sebastian. It was on this highway, my hosts had told me, that I would be safe for Santander and on it I would find stations for trains, and stops for buses. It was precisely four pm when we arrived at Zarauz. We stopped outside the tourist information bureau at the exact moment that Senora appeared with office keys, after siesta. The only map she could let me have was one covering the whole of Spain and showing all the Paradors. I had worked from a small scale map of the whole of France since running out of Brittany, and I was happy to take this one, even though the Mediter- ranean and Portugal were not presently on our agenda as destinations — but they would always keep.

On and on we grafted, pausing now and then to drink hot water from a plastic bottle carried in the left rear pannier pocket — now with a map of Spain for company. Here, this was the only available treatment when dehydration set in. We did not pass premises where cold beer flowed — from either tap or bottle.

Some forty kilometres out of San Sebastian night started to drop, quickly and suddenly; so much so, that I worried about my view of the road, forced as I was to share it with so many dangerously driven cars lit by high beam headlights, never dipped, and controlled seemingly by drivers on the edges of fury and combustion.

We had just zoomed down a vicious, winding, mountain pass at a speed too great with brakes at smoking point, when I made a shockingly bad gear change, shifting through all fifteen (from top to bottom) and jammed the chain on the dérailleur. I had asked too much of the mechanism. It was locked solid. I swore at myself repeatedly. I lifted vélo off the road and into a safe shallow ditch at the side, and inspected the trouble by the light of our faithful old detachable battery powered headlamp. I lifted the back wheel and pedalled by hand. In so doing, I released the chain from the teeth, and saw that it was unlinked — broken and disconnected. In these dark, brooding Atlantic Pyrenees we were now without the essential endless belt of metal: powerless — and not for the first time. I made a miserable, pessimistic prediction that it was not the last, either. I remembered (from a previous holiday) the long, chainless, free-wheel and walk to St. Paul de Léon in far off Brittany and the vélo carrying walk, without free-wheel, to Concarneau with an airless back tyre earlier on our present journey.

Shining the lamp at the ditch, I was pleased to see litter. There was a large, empty, greasy potato crisp bag which I picked up, and with another piece of waste paper (I preferred not to think about its original function) I hauled the chain off the cogs and slid the oily, severed steel snake into the thrown away plastic sack; and packed the precious parcel in the right front pannier case.

I looked at the map of all of Spain in the torch's light, worried that I might drop and break it too. I estimated that we were about eight kilometres from the nearest help at a coastal town called Deva. We had been in this kind of pickle before, but in France, where I could at least communicate in my way. Here, and now, I felt cast off in this isolation, and for a few minutes watched the wretched impatient world race by, and with dirty, shaking hands, rolled a sorry one in the ditch. I cursed the self-inflicted predicament we were in. Would I ever learn to control the gear levers properly?

We started the steep climb. At the summit of this mountain, I saw, with the moon's aid, a pyramid of twinkling scrap motor-cars piled on top of each other. I put vélo on its stand at the sloped entrance to the vehicle funeral parlour of a junk yard, and was greeted by three, on duty, suspicious, German Shepherds. Five people were talking animatedly in the darkness. I stood at the cordon sanitaire drawn by the dogs, coughing, humming and whistling. I was not getting through — and oddly, the dogs were not barking. I went on making noises, and after about ten minutes, Senora left the group — my crude, attention getting efforts had paid off at last. She appeared to me, walking slowly up the incline.

Concocting a suitably woebegone expression, I asked her if she spoke French. No — with a sideways head shake. English? Likewise. Now using body language (there was no other) as obsequiously as I could contrive, I pointed to the chainless cogs, front and back. Middle-aged, and with a kind face, she sighed loudly and sauntered back to the men folk.

At first I thought that no further interest would be shown to me. It seemed as if she was not even reporting my predicament to them. It was probably best in that case to have a roll up and move on. The brakes were all right, and we had a bit of I.O.U. downhill to come. Just as I started rummaging about for pouch, holder, papers and lighter, one of the men walked up at an even more leisurely pace than Senora. As he approached, he discharged the dogs. Even in the near dark, I could see that Senor wore gold framed glasses, a Hitler moustache, and no hair. His boiler suit was made of oil. We could not speak to each other.

After we had wiped our hands on the wad of cotton waste he had invited me to share, I took out the crisp bag and poured the parted chain onto the ground. With many sighs and shrugs, and pointing to his dead cars, I knew he wished me to understand that his business and expertise had to do with things that moved on four wheels, and not two. He held up four fingers, and then put a thumb up. He held up two fingers and then put a thumb down. He mimed very effectively

138

the hands on steering-wheel, the feet on clutch and brake pedal, the going through the gearbox, the correct use of mirror. Had I been carefree, I would have enjoyed and appreciated his wordless, one man, show.

I took out of my shorts pocket the three charcoal grey sheets of kitchen paper towelling which had served me well for weeks as handkerchiefs, and put them to my eyes. I looked at the now clear sky and stars, and at my feet, and sighed until he left. He stopped, turned around, and looked at me squintingly in the gloaming. A few metres away there was a rubbish skip, and putting my arms on top of it, and keeping the filthy sheets of tissue pressed to my eyes, I committed my head to the rim of the noxious container, and stayed still. I heard Senor walk on, and the sound of his indignant muttering faded. I did not expect to see him again, but waited just in case.

He rejoined Senora and the others, and then disappeared. When he reappeared he was carrying what to a person with breathing difficulty, would have been a supply of life-saving oxygen. It was a toolbag. With a horrible fawning grin I clapped him, but he took no bow. Unknown to me, when he had first looked at the chain, he had discovered that the link, which had given way when I had immobilised the gearing, was neither broken nor lost – merely slipped: it was still halfway on the chain but out of its housing.

The great man started. He had brought his own much more powerful torch. I gripped the vélo firmly but at first did not look at what he was doing. Star gazing, I tried to think about time and the distance as a bicycle ride between Alpha Centauri and the North (Pole) Star. When I did glance down, I saw that strewn upon the ground were hammers, pliers, pincers and other instruments – oily and glistening in the torch light. Senor spoke (but not to me) all the time. I guessed that he was swearing, and that this, if declared in the Confessional, might have drawn strong remarks and extra penance. Half an hour later the chain had been reconnected but outside the frame. He stood up and profaned. Ventilated, he started all over again. After another heart-aching half hour, the chain was, for the second time, joined up, inside the frame and on the cogs. After a short trial spin – going through all the gears — I sang and laughed. I gave Senor an extended standing ovation, calling Senora, and the rest of them still talking in the yard, to witness what had been done by their improvising genius.

With left thumb and forefinger rubbing together, and eyebrows benignly raised, I signalled the international, silent reference to money. Senor generously passed me his cotton waste wad again, and asked for the equivalent of two pounds and fifty pence — which I gratefully doubled. We were on our so far undefeated way — heading for Deva. The repair has endured for more than three thousand kilometres. The chain and I have not troubled each other since that night on the N634 in northern Spain.

Happy, but tired, I wanted to park somewhere with lots of food, drink and sleep. About four kilometres on from the scrap yard saviour's premises, I saw a sign shining in the darkness — Hotel/Restaurant. Knowing that I would hear the word 'completo' when asking for a bed, I went into the bar. It was ten pm. The room was empty. Senor, in charge, had a memorably benevolent face. Sympatico.

He smiled and was full of goodwill. "Inglese?" he asked, and when I nodded, "Momento." He left and returned with his nephew, a student, reading English. The young man was on holiday, working for his uncle in the kitchen. His English was sound, and he came across as a thoroughly pleasant and helpful person. Having confirmed that all rooms were full, the nephew suggested that I could put my sleeping-bag in the garage, sharing with the dog. Yes, I could certainly have dinner, and no, there was not any draught beer, but plenty of cold bottles for which I instantly settled.

Uncle and nephew thought more about the garage plan and judged, on reflection, that the dog would not think much of the scheme. In which case, neither would I. As a safer alternative, they proposed the barn at the back of the building. This was open at the sides, built on dry sloping mud, and it housed rusty farm implements and vehicles, cobwebs, and a fair amount of land and airborne wildlife. I spotted a relatively level area, brought vélo round, put the sleeping-bag inside the bivouac — ready for the night — and returned to the bar for more beer and dinner.

The dining-room was now filling and noisy, but the good nephew, who had temporarily abandoned his work, looked after me in an exemplary manner, speaking (and showing off) his English gleefully. Steering me to a table for four, he whipped off the three other place settings, and bore wine in an immense carafe with a large no nonsense all purpose glass. He chose, as his principle topic of conversation, the issue of Basque separatism pleading the case for his cause with eloquent passion. I left the menu choices to him, and in between checking that the Tinto level in my glass was always high, he served a most appetising soup in a huge bowl, and then brought succulent, bone surgery free fish, and followed up with several sharp cheeses.

With hunger and thirst out of the way, and mellow, I went back to the bar for coffee and digestifs. At that hour the place was heavily full, but the excellent nephew again gave me preferred service. I gladly gave ear to the next part of his speech in which he rounded on those who thought that all Basques were bombers and shooters. "We only want our country, as you only want your bicycle. Is either of us asking for that which is not his?" Part of my daily radio work at the time was to field questions and material like this on the air. I was not going to allow an intelligent and charming young Basque to put me back to work prematurely. He was plainly a natural debater, and expected me to challenge. I was about to explain that the subject matter sounded too much like work, when the television saved me. Everyone in the bar turned to a large set in the corner when a Basque game got underway. It looked like a mixture of long range five's and squash, with players coming to, and going off the court, all the time. I asked nephew to explain the rudiments which he did between delighted yells, and disappointed groans, in unison with his uncle's customers. It was a local derby needle match. I identified the proper team and made as much noise as any, but was not sure if our side, in the end, had won or lost.

Churchill's Hendaye holiday also included a visit to an important match. It bored him, and he walked off annoyed that this had been arranged by people who should have been aware that 'I hate all games'. This had upset the spectators —

enough for him to return to the court three quarters of an hour later.

By now the WC, for use by bar and restaurant customers, and the only washing facility available to me, was constantly full, and flushing non-stop. Rather than ask for anything else, I decided to ditch teeth cleaning and other ablutions. Instead I went to my pitch in the barn content to be the guest of roosting birds and roving rodents. I forced myself to regard them, when I made the familiar ripping noise on the sleeping-bag zip, as friends and room mates for the night.

Such sleep as I could get was bumpy. I went from hillock to hillock − now sliding, now corkscrewing, seeking a kinder area of plain. Without exhaustion and large quantities of food and drink, I would have been awake until the birds sounded reveille; but some unconsciousness must have come, because when I finally gave up, as the dawn chorus began, I was aware of some dreadful, themeless, dreaming.

At about eight am. Senor uncle (of the benign, sympathetic face) was once again ready for business, and gracefully ushered me to the WC door where he silently demonstrated the opening and closing of taps, the washing of face, the brushing of teeth. I did all this peacefully in the freshly cleaned convenience, and was then ready for lots of life restoring coffee. I put the wash bag and towel on a chair, and had coffee with a piece of cake, sitting on a stool at the bar.

A young couple came in, the girl also with bag and towel. She looked at my things with knowing reassurance, and smiling, I pointed to the door. The man was bearded, thick set, wore steel rimmed glasses, and was in great need of coffee. When the girl had finished in the WC, the three of us started talking, and exchanged our news as we would have done in the deserts of Arabia. They were Germans on a journey of mutual commodiousness. He was a professional driver, and his current mission was to deliver a large transit van from Germany to the western mediterranean. The girl, whose destination was a campsite forty kilometres the other side of Santander, where she was to join friends, was an acquaintance of the driver, not lover − a distinction that she was keen to establish − and she was glad to have this handy,

142

well timed lift.

She was blonde, teutonically archetypal and attractive, in excellent condition, glowing with physical fitness. I was not at all surprised to learn that she was training to be a PE teacher. This vehicle, she explained (pointing in its direction), was quite big enough for them to have a mattress each on the floor.

"Not a great double one, you understand."

She seemed anxious (I knew not why) that I should be convinced that there was nothing connubial between them.

"Two single ones. One for him. One for me."

Herr driver was indifferent to all this, and had nothing to contribute. I asked him how long it would take them to reach Santander from where we were.

"About four and a half hours," he replied, and pulled happily on his cigar.

Four and a half hours. I told Satan to get well behind me. Several times. I was nursing bad, incorrect, thoughts. It was touch and go as to whether I would fall into the unspeakable. He had already told me that the vehicle in his charge was fitted to carry up to four bicycles: and I had enough cash on me to make a good contribution towards the diesel.

"Four bicycles?"

"Ja, four bicycles."

Hmmmm. Hmmmm. Diablo was closing at a dangerous rate. We did some two way mind reading. My eyes went from vélo (perched outside, packed, and ready for the off) to transit van; from transit van to vélo, and back to the faces of my new found coffee neighbours. I gave the devil a good kick, increased the distance between us, and changed the subject to tennis. I suggested that they must have been pleased with the outcome of that year's Wimbledon when two Germans, Stich and Graf had won. I asked for the correct way to pronounce the former's name.

Suddenly the girl went to the vehicle and returned with a map of the region we were in. She showed me the precise location of her campsite. She had unfolded, and spread it out, on one of the tables. Herr driver stayed at the bar with his third cup of coffee and cigars, while she and I poured over the cartography. It was difficult to keep my eyes on the road. She was wearing an overloose tee-shirt of miniskirt length. Her enchanting, honey bronzed breasts, were quite unconfined. Once she looked quickly at me ogling her, and leant over even more, pointing with lovely slender fingers and beautiful nails, to choices of routes. I cannot remember a word of whatever it was that we discussed. Slowly, she folded the map. With all my limited willpower I paid the bill, said farewell to the German couple, and left for more mountaineering.

Gasping in the intense morning heat, I approached the next peak, looking forward to a fast, cooling, air flowing downhill run. The German transit van overtook us, but it was too hazardous to wave, as we were at high speed on a nasty bend. A few minutes later, going up hill again but on a stretch of straight road, the van came back, moving slowly in the opposite direction, as if searching for something or someone. It must be them. They had decided to take us to Santander. Weakness would win over will after all. I was sure that they were looking for a place to turn, and would then pick us up. We would reach our final destination in about four hours. They would persuade me to end my self-inflicted misery. I would not resist.

Parking at the roadside while I waited for them, I broke out the pouch, made a sweaty one, and fantasised about the next few hours. Vélo would be stowed securely on a special rack, and I would be on the front bench seat, map reading, with the girl beside me. Of course our objective had been reached when we arrived in San Sebastian. Mission definitely accomplished. Miguel unquestionably right. What an agreeable, triumphant way to arrive at the ferry terminal. This was Fate's work. It had intervened, insisting that the lift should be a well deserved gratuity. Half an hour passed, no white transit van had slowed and stopped for us. I wondered why. It should have been obvious, much sooner, that theirs was not the only vehicle of its kind with 'D' for Germany on these Basque mountain roads. I told Fate to go to hell, and to stop playing games.

Slowly and wearily we went on. I mulled over the previous night in the barn, for which Senor uncle had made no charge. I ruminated on what the night to come had in mind for us.

144

We descended into Deva. On the third bay, risen above the sea, there was an inn with rooms, but there was no room. Completo. We rode quietly along the beach front road, intimidated by the sight of the corniche and high mountains on all sides. I felt locked up: hemmed in. I had sensed this once in Vancouver, British Columbia, western Canada. There, looking out of a window one day, I saw Grouse Mountain and the foothills of the Rockies; and the sea. Nothing else. There was no way out. And it was like that here in Deva. Brainscanningly claustrophobic.

We should go through life (I was told long ago) expecting God always to have a custard pie or two up His sleeve. He had had some good sport already this day and now He let go with another platter of splotch. The road at the end of the beach took us left towards the town across a railway level-crossing — and to the station. There, at rest, was a train waiting with open doors to take us to Bilbao. There was a bus type sign saying so at the front. Bicycles were already on board, taking it easy in the guard's van. I had money for a ticket. At Bilbao, there would be another train for Santander. Just as Miguel and Anita had explained to me in San Sebastian. This one looked very much like a BR regional sprinter, and from its comfortable seating the mountains would be a pleasure to view — to look up to. The road ahead was flat and clear. We accelerated, and in highest gear, fled out of town like fugitives.

Staying on the N634 we (vélo and I) slowly and painfully hairpinned our way up, and ecstatically free-wheeled our way down, these sheer, coastal ranges towards Durango in the high heat of August. An hour or so after Deva, more and more police were sharing the road with us. Their cars and motor-cycles sped up and down both ways, with sirens screaming and flashing lights blinding. I assumed that there had been some terrorist activity, and was prepared to be challenged, questioned, and probably diverted.

The motor-cycle mounted police riders resembled the late General George (Blood and Guts) Patton in dress and manner. Large, gold helmeted, breeched, full buttocked, gaitored and revolvered, they swaggered as they rode. Whatever the reason for their widespread presence, it was clearly a

145

big story. Radio, TV, and newspaper vehicles joined in, also dashing up and down. Instinctively, I supposed to myself, I should find a 'phone and feed whatever it was to the radio station in Plymouth. Better still, perhaps I could flag down one of the radio cars on the road and do the business with their help and favour. On reflection (lasting about a tenth of a second) I decided to have nothing to do with it. We carried on with our mission. Operation Oblivious.

Eventually, we were stopped near the top of a mountain, at the outskirts of a small town. A policeman in bright red and blue walked across the road and pointed to the vélo. Surely we were not the quarry of this frenzied search? The raison d'etre for this imposing application of police power? Why had they not taken us out an hour ago? Why had they waited so long? There was nothing in the officer's bearing to suggest that he regarded himself as man of the match — that he had netted the big one. I still had no idea what this was all about. Then I saw a few other cyclists leg stretching on the verge — and the dinero dropped. This was the day of the annual 'San Sebastian Classic' cycle race. A one day version of the Tour de France, on a run of two hundred and thirty-eight kilometres. I should have been aware — there had been much talk of the event in San Sebastian. Automatically, every year the first ten competitors to finish the Tour de France are invited to take their places in this tourney. Talking in sign language, the policeman said that we would be delayed for half an hour, while the road was cleared for the supermen. We were held for ninety minutes.

Soon came the commercial sponsorship and media cars in fast convoy. They raced through, although one press vehicle stopped, and self-important looking people got out, displayed themselves, and went on. Then the great company of champion riders came into view. Preceded by a cavalcade of loudspeaker vans, with winking lights and advertising logos, the sultans of saddle sweatlessly propelled their parallelograms up the sloping, snaking, hill.

When all had passed, the police nodded us on. As we got under heavy way again, I went over my thoughts when we were first stopped. The stomach churned and went cold, as

146

the brightly attired policeman halted us with a raised tree trunk of an arm. We were not on an auto pista; was it a passport check? Did one need a special riding licence or permit in Spain? Were helmets compulsory? I shrank from the prospect of any dealings with Spanish traffic officials. British motorists had told me that life changes abruptly when they take up the subject of road and driving laws. However, there was no crisis, and during the enforced stop, I mixed some Spanish tobacco with the English variety I had been using, having long ago run out of the special pipe type shag which I have been enjoying for many years. This Euro-nic-mix in my pouch was not a success, and unusually, I coughed. Wrapping the mélange in tissue, I put it away, for use only in real emergency and thenceforth used Old Holborn on its own.

The N634 was taking us well inland to Durango, and I missed the closeness of the sea, but I was determined that we should not lose sight of this road. By holding to it, we would get to Santander. O blessed place with its ferry terminal and vessel back to Plymouth. But would there be, in the middle of August, without a reservation, space for us? Bad, negative, defeatist thoughts took hold again and I rued the cause of my present misery: the drunken drive in 1981. I wished that the bicycle had never been invented. Falling down, and plodding up these cruel hills, I craved a flat earth where we could effortlessly engage our top gear, pumping a little easy muscle power onto the pedals, to make good, untroubled tireless time, dreaming, whistling, and singing along. I was sure that there was not a plain in Spain. There was not even a Salisbury Plain. There were no flat lands anywhere. This planet was not flat. There was no level ground. Horizontal surfaces were tricks of mirages. I would not be joining the Flat Earth Society.

Too wretchedly unhappy now even to raise a tune, I planned, when in Durango, to hire a taxi or other vehicle to take us only as far as Bilbao, and there to find a ship, any ship, bound for anywhere in the UK, and then by train we would return to Plymouth. I dismissed all thoughts of a landfall in the South West. Aberdeen would do nicely.

After several sweaty hours, relieved only slightly by

frequent hot water swigging stops, I saw the buildings of Durango and felt better. No more would I pack and unpack the panniers, stuffing and unstuffing them with disgusting, dirty clothes. No more would I worry about chain oil, and the hardness of the tyres. Aboard a UK bound ship out of Bilbao there would be running water, perhaps a table cloth, and quiet, sea-lulled sleep upon a bunk. Our long trip was over.

It was about five in the afternoon when we made a final roll down, and into, Durango, but not before I had seen, just outside the town, a matchbox type hotel with one car parked near the entrance. There must have been space for us. There was plenty. I then realised that the place was shut, either for the holiday season, or receivership. It was yet another tourists' dead duck — in the middle of August. I found this impossible to understand, and as there was no one to talk to, we rode on, unenlightened. Ahead of me, also on a bicycle, a youngster (an early teenager I judged) fell behind me for about the tenth time. He had been overtaking and slowing for about half an hour. Maybe he had been putting down a race gauntlet. Perchance he had also seen the San Sebastian Classic. I was neither alarmed nor particularly interested in his riding, and when I turned left into the town, he went straight on.

The time was a quarter past five in the afternoon of Saturday, August 11th. The town was quiet. Few people were about. I looked for a bar — always a source of local knowledge as my hosts in San Sebastian had stressed. "In such places," Miguel had said, "you will find all the intelligence you need to do with accommodation — and everything else." That item came second on the agenda. First, the slaking of unbearable thirst. A supply of cold beer in large glasses superseded all other needs.

I had three of those but only tasted the last one. When I signalled for the fourth, I was ready for business — but could not conduct it. Sadly, nothing could be done because nothing could be said. Owners and customers had neither English nor French. Dispirited and frustrated, I longed for just a few words of Spanish or better still, a phrase book. I had neither.

Hydrated and fortified, I looked for another bar where I might find a French or English speaker. As we rode slowly along a street which presumably was in, or near, the town centre, the young cyclist of the main road re-emerged. Enquiringly he spoke the word "Hotel?" I nodded enthusiastically, and said "si" and "gracias" several times. He motioned me to follow him, and I wondered where our ride would end. There was a moment of disquiet of the kind that came to me when I was rescued by the council workers near Biarritz. Had I been duped? Would bad people rob, wound, or even kill? But my need for the solace of a mattress, with or without sheets, was great and I took the risk – if there was one. This teenager did not look devilish. He was a cyclist, and cyclists are good; and I was yet to sleep in a Spanish bed. So far there had been three nights, two on the floor in San Sebastian, one in a barn near Deva.

Our young guide took us along a one way street the wrong, illegal way. It was empty, but soon we were loudly cursed by screeching Senora who hectored and lectured from the balcony of her third floor apartment. She was quite apoplectic, but the boy, perhaps not for the first time, heard it out uncomprehendingly. I copied but expected to be hunted down by the sounds of police cars. She was in such a choleric condition that we could still receive her loud and clear, when well out of sight and riding lawfully again.

I could not fathom this adolescent's interest in me. If he was an aspiring professional cyclist, I was hardly the ideal coach. A base theory came to mind. Was this youth, by chance, an apprentice pimp? Were we on our way to a bordello? Were we bawdy house bound? No. His help was entirely well meant. As we turned a corner he pointed ahead, and to the right, where the word 'HOTEL' was displayed in big lettering on a swaying sign. He left me and I shouted my gracias.

It was an oldish building with a large pleasant garden, and a drinks' terrace above. I parked vélo by a fish pond, and went up the steps and through a grand entrance. Senor appeared in morning dress, superintending a wedding reception. I, reeking, asked if he had a spare room, garage or potting shed.

"Room? Completo. Garage? Completo. Patting shid? Completo."

Bad news, but he did have some English. Despondent, I asked if he served draught beer in the bar. No. I went to the counter inside, where a mournful fellow with a lopsidedly dejected moustache, opened a bottle of beer in slow motion.

There was a depressing atmosphere in the room. The sorrowful looking drinkers wore suits, draining the last of the wedding wine while I, a disinterested third party, quickly got the message. A knot had been tied earlier in the day. The guests were not celebrating the occasion. Conversation was muted. There was no hint of fiesta. Not wishing by my presence to add to their misery, I called for another glass of bottled beer, and took it to the terrace where I joined a second cluster of melancholy supporters. They had found a way. Inside were 'HIS', outside 'HERS'. The teams wore either red or white buttonholes, and by keeping apart, had found the only modus vivendi for survival on the day.

Making eye contact with one of the mourners on the bride's side who spoke a bit of French, I asked for directions to the nearest draught beer. This diverted him from his grief, and there was a sign of brightness as he drew a map on the once white plastic table, fore-fingering his way through tobacco and spilled drink.

He had sketched well, and I found the bar he recommended easily. It was crowded with young people who talked, and played their bar games, noisily. This made me nervous, but I was soothed by the smiles and calm of two corkingly beautiful girls behind the bar. What I wanted primarily was a place with running water, and a level surface for sleep. Then, refreshed and clean, I would see about road transport to Bilbao and the sea voyage back to Britain. My mind was not working well, and recurring bouts of wooziness let me know that I was overdrawn at the energy bank. One of the girls spoke some French, and the other some English. I told them my news, and my troubles. They called out to a young man in dark glasses who left his bar game and came over.

Every drinking spot in the world seems to have one. A king at the top of the local street cred and fixit league. With sign language and bits of pidgin Spanish, French and English, he indicated that he understood, and took over my life. He relieved the girls at the bar who then left. They were being ordered out on reconnaissance, and reported back half an hour later. There was a place to which Senor Fixito would now take me – we would both ride. I was much touched by the trouble they had all taken, but the female bicycle my new leader was to mount had a flat rear tyre. We tried various pumps (permps) mine included, but nothing worked. One of the girls was sent on a borrowing mission in the neighbourhood, and I returned to the bar for another refreshing glass of cold beer on tap, and a second saucer of olives.

With air at last in the tyre, we rode off in single file, and after many turns to right and left, we arrived at a restaurant where Senor, dressed in full kitchen white, gravely confirmed that I could dine and sleep in his establishment. Nosh and kip were in the bag and I was very pleased – with life in general, and in particular with the people of Durango. Senor Restauranto also allowed me to park vélo safely in the kitchen surrounds, and then after thanking young Senor Fixito, I was taken to another building (where after using three different keys – one for the main door, one for the floor and one for the room) I was led to a cell like space with a barred window giving a perfect, panoramic view of the fire escape. Against one wall there was a bit of ancient upholstered furniture standing on four legs. I decided that the contrivance had once been a bed. When I tried it, the mattress groaned. It surrendered horribly, embracing and engulfing me in the bottom of a deep valley. However, there was a wash basin, shaver plug, and bathroom, all on the same floor.

My host told me that I could have dinner at any time after seven thirty pm. It was now six o'clock, and I longed to lie for an hour, bathe, do a little laundry, eat and then sleep again. I lay in the ravine of broken springs, too tired to remove even footwear, and woke seven hours later at one o'clock in the morning – in what I believe was a kind of travellers' hostel. The taste in my mouth was corrosively foul, and although craving more sleep, I also felt great hunger. I much regretted missing Senor's table – by all sign language accounts, it was popular with every gourmand in town. Too fatigued to shower, I cleaned the teeth, and passed out again — waking at nine. This gave me an aggregate of more than fourteen hours. My nervous system had not been inactive for so long since infancy, when on one occasion (I was told) someone swapped my syrup of figs for whisky.

Gone now though was all yesterday's shameful defeatism. How could I possibly have thought so wetly about trucks to, and ships from, Bilbao? I managed to key myself out of the building and went to Senor's bar for several cups of milky coffee and a slice of cold tapas egg and bacon pie — as good as any in Devon childhood days.

Leading vélo out onto the road, I looked with competitive panache at the mountains all around us, and imitating the darts match official, roared "Game On" at them — tenacious in my determination that we should have a good hard go at each other this day, or, at any rate, for as long as we could last. On leaving Durango that Sunday morning, I was in vigour — and full of it. As we made way, I could still hear loud talk from the bar where one of Senor's sons, as if on roller-skates, slid between many coffee machines, dispensing to a congregation of pre-church going faithful. I supposed that they would be quieter at Mass. Church bells pealed, and we carried the sounds for a long time after leaving Durango in the hot, windless forenoon.

Chapter Fourteen

We resumed our mountain combat, now hurtling down, now struggling and panting up in lowest gear, now gaspingly labouring on foot, always wanting the hurtful gravity, and sound of cars, to end.

Some three and a half hours after Durango, clouds of dark, reddish smoke rose ahead. Bilbao, it must be Bilbao. Steel town on the north coast. All I knew about the place was that it was a seat of the Basque autonomous Government in 1936/7 during the Civil War. It is a port with a population of nearly half a million, with wine exports, iron ore, steel and ship building being principal industries.

As we closed on the industrial haze, Middlesborough — steel town on the north east coast — came into my mental focus. Like Bilbao, it too has a transporter bridge across water. I saw the Teeside conurbation on joining my first ship. The vessel merged with the low mountain of pinkish brown iron ore surrounding it. There was the overcast of mineral dust, and my concern for the state of a brand new brass bound uniform — shortly replaced by a boiler suit. Sea training began that afternoon after an all night train crawl from Plymouth via London and Darlington. A Spanish steward, Kojak bald, wearing a rusty white coat. The 'riggers', finding a way to get my steamer trunk and other gear on to the deck of the empty, high-sided ship without a gangway. The only way up and down was on a long, steeply inclined, quivering ladder.

The business of getting into the berth; 'cabin' was not the mot juste. No key. "The other cadet must have taken it with him on leave," — from the relief second mate. The unscrewing of the brass ventilator fitted to the door: the arm going through the hole, and the reach down to the lock. So little space.

"Is this where we put our gear, Sir."

"This is where you put your gear, and where two of you live, sleep and study. Now get your glad rags on, and pump up the bridge fresh water tank."

Meeting the semi-rotary pump handle by the galley for the first of many workings, the instruction on priming, and the looking up at the tank for overflow, and rest.

Different shaped and much larger ships came into view as we made our steady approach into Bilbao. The navigation was fairly straightforward, but the passage was interminable. It took us two and a half hours in the choking, furnace-like air to clear the heavily built-up zone. Once, a following car sounded its horn incessantly. I assumed that this did not concern us, as we were behaving prudently. Several minutes later, we were to learn that a certain motorist did not agree. He had been trying to overtake us for some time, and when eventually he did, pulled over, stopped, got out, and strode irately towards us. From his gesticulations, raised voice, and constant use of the word 'SOLO', I gathered that he was charging us with using the road as if it had been designed and built for our sole, personal, and exclusive use. This upset and perplexed me — I was controlling vélo in the normal way, and it was the first rebuke that I had been obliged to undergo on the trip from another road user. I looked at him peacefully, heard out his tirade, and offered my hand. After careful consultation with himself, he grudgingly took it, and we both resumed our journeys, driving and riding exactly as before. Soon after this, we cleared Bilbao and saw for the first time, a road sign for Santander. There was an instant surge of energy, and we went faster.

Once at the start of a particularly long climb, there came the shouted, jarring sound of an unlovely British voice. It originated from the open window of a red GB plated car coming down the mountain at great speed, going in the opposite direction.

"Why don't you get off and walk?" it wanted to know.

Ignoring the rasping impertinence, I wondered what life

154

had done to this grating Briton, and assumed that had I been walking, he would have shouted, 'Why don't you get on and ride?' Why the gratuitous rudeness – or was my sense of humour, or lack of it, at fault? At that moment, I could have done with enlightenment from the zoologist Desmond Morris: he would have explained it all. But I did not know then, that I should be indebted to this individual who could prove that empty vessels make the most noise.

We stopped in as many little towns and villages as possible for rest and hydration, although there were not that many populated areas in these parts. In one, we had a prolonged stop and a lengthy conversation with one of two sisters, who, with mother, ran the bar. The contrast in the siblings' looks was remarkable. The older one was memorably, classically, attractive; the younger, strikingly plain: but it was she, a warm and beckoning young woman, who was keen to speak English. She suggested a few ideas as to where we might spend the night, and we looked at her wall map together.

As early evening began to cool the day, we arrived at a place, in a valley, so small that I could not remember its name from Senorita's briefing, and I had memorised all the proper names we were likely to reach that day. One of the houses, in what was really an overgrown hamlet, had a Coca Cola sign outside, and I had enough Spanish practice by now to know that it would therefore also be a bar. Deceptively large inside, with a games and function room, it was owned by a quarrelling couple. Senora was dark, youngish, and attractive, with brown eyes afire. Senor, stocky, red and rustic, tractor-like and brooding, went to and fro his farm fields in the intervals between shouting matches with his lady.

A few local people in the bar watched the television, wine and tapas to hand – unmindful of the war. Once, during a longish cease fire, I put it (in body language) to Senora that if the function-cum-games room was not in use that night, I could put down my sleeping-bag and bivouac there – for a consideration. She gave her agreement, together with permission to park vélo in the same space. The WC facilities were also handy, working and clean.

My mind, after I had done this, was easy, and I tucked in to a large plate of tapas and local wine for dinner. At about ten o'clock, Senor came in for the last time that day, beaten by the light. Senora must have mentioned in a previous skirmish my intentions for the night, because I heard the word 'bicycletto' several times — with growing fortissimo. It was clear that Senor had changed his mind and heart. He now took the opposite view: namely that when it came to Inglese and bicycletto and sleeping on the games room floor, Senora did not understand house policy. A last shout, and he went out again in the darkness to his fields — perhaps to kick a scarecrow. He and I have not met since, so I will never be sure. Senora then gave me the heave-ho, jerking her left, beautiful, and slender thumb, doorwards. I packed up the sleeping gear, secured it to vélo, and we were back in the dark on the long uphill road, bound for Castro Urdiales. The names made me think of Cuba and the Northern Lights.

The barren land showed no hospitality signs. At no time had I felt more apprehensively alone, and lonely, than on this winding road that black and starless night. There were no lights from any compass points in the sky. Only from earthly machines moving fast. Motor vehicles of all kinds from many different countries roared and switch-backed their way along the S bends and hairpins. After more than an hour of walking the vélo, both up and down — I was too frightened to ride — my spirits were at rock bottom low, breaking all records to date. It was now almost midnight, and I was worried, tired and depressed. I could not recall a time when I had been more fed up.

As we reached yet another summit, and the outskirts of a town some ten kilometres from Castro Urdiales, I saw a brightly lit neon red cross on the right. The smallish one storey building looked like a first aid post, and I stopped at the front entrance. It seemed to be unoccupied, but a light shone from the back on to a piece of rough, stone and parched grass covered, ground. I wheeled vélo round and parked, observing that the surface was fairly flat. I off-loaded the sleeping-bag and bivvy and arranging them, knew that this was journey's end for the day. As I unzipped, and unbuttoned, I must have been seen by at least one person moving around in the well lit back room. I froze and expected the worst — perhaps a challenge for trespass, or even something more felonious. The light went out. I stood still and waited, playing back to myself grisly things that I had been told, and read, about Spanish prisons. I heard the sound of a key turning in its lock. I listened for footsteps. There was no sound. No one came to me. I rolled a cigarette, and spent several more minutes anticipating arrest. The person in the building would either have 'phoned the police or driven to them. We were in the heart of Basque country, and I could not allow myself to believe that having been spotted in such suspicious circumstances, a cyclist would be left to rest in peace. But, mercifully, I was not troubled. The night was so hot that I used my sleeping gear as ground sheets only.

Small stones, and invisible animal life thwarted slumber, but at least the lying down, and spells of almost lost consciousness, revived me a little when I packed up at sunrise. By looking at a window, I could see enough of my face to guide the cell charged razor, and to have a passable shave.

In the small town a few minutes ride on, one café was open in the early morning. It was dirty, overrun by flies and cockroaches, and only two other people were in it. Such was my need for coffee, that I could not have cared much if the insects had chosen to paddle on top of the expresso in my cup. It took Senor five minutes to acknowledge me as I stood at the bar, another two to produce the creamy drink, another one to put a small cake upon a chipped plate. I timed this by pretending to be in a hurry, as I looked impatiently at my watch.

After two cups, I braved the WC, wash bag in hand. It was awkward in this wet, cramped, paper strewn space, to put water on face, and dentifrice on teeth. I had been struggling for about ten minutes, when there was a battering on the door and an impatient caballero asked, loudly demanded, how much longer I was going to be. Presumably that was the purpose of his visit. I gave up, and came out to find no one in the café other than Senor, who surely must have had his own private facilities. If he had been the door basher, I would not have recognised the voice. He had taken a daytime vow of silence. He made not a sound, spoke not a word, as I settled up for four cups of coffee and a small piece of cake. Nor did he say anything to anybody else. He was on the wrong shift, and would have found existence more bearable working owls' rather than larks' hours.

Clearly he spoke only after sunset. After sunrise, manifestly, he dealt with the world by pen — writing on greasy scraps of paper, and speaking through sighs. I had now collected two more of life's mysteries, never to be unravelled. Who was the person in the Red Cross post, and why did he or she leave me alone? Who was the phantom WC door knocker and what was his urgency?

Scratching a bit, I remounted vélo and we headed off to Castro Urdiales. It was an hour away for us, up and down the unforgiving mountain range. As we made our final descent, the resort showed itself — a good-looking town, with a wide amount of stretching, sandy beach. Many expensive façaded hotels had been built on the sea front, and the cafés and restaurants were packed as we rode by in the morning heat. I had turned into Castro Urdiales seeking money and tobacco. Both were hard to find. After mistaking or mistaken, directions, I found a tobacconist on the seashore road, where the atmosphere was not unlike that in some British betting shops. Expressions on both sides of the counter were gloomily pensive, and it took Senor a long time to pass me, one at a time, the three large pouches of hand rolling tobacco that I had grinningly pointed to in the dark room.

Now for a bank. I had spotted one a few doors from the funereal tobacco shop. It wore the heraldry of Visa and Access, and I went through the necessary rigmarole of getting to the wallet via a plastic bag in a holdall with straps, lashed on top of the sleeping equipment on the vélo's back bracket. Avoiding the cash tills, I caught the eye of a man at the office side who came with me to the entrance where the machines lived.

I dealt him both Visa and Access. He nodded, and took the latter, feeding it into the monster's open, expectant, mouth. The card was swallowed, gulped — I heard an eructation — the bank man asked me how much I wanted. I put in for the equivalent of one hundred pounds, but told him that I had no secret PIN digits for this card. He ignored me and started pushing buttons. Nothing happened. There were no lights, nor more digestive noises. Then we both saw the 'OUT OF ORDER' sign. My luck had run away. At last it had happened — the theft of a magic money card in a foreign country. I would never see it again. It would have an eternal rest home in a computer's colon. I looked at bank man and groaned: and started hopping on one leg at a time. He, though, was calm and made a soothing gesture with arms outstretched, and palms down. Bishop like, he signalled me to kneel, or sit on a nearby chair. His hands were steady. He did more button touching. There was no response. I looked hopefully at ceiling lights to see if there had been a power cut, but they were bright. I stood up but was reseated by Senor bank man, the last person in the world to have seen my priceless plastic. He turned back to the machine — hands prayerfully together. I arranged mine devoutly as well, and waited, aware that I did not know how to report this grievous loss to the card's headquarters in Southend-on-Sea.

Suddenly there was a whine — my own was soundless. The gizmology, having tasted the card, rejected the flavour and decided to spew out. I leapt in the air, and clutched it tightly, and tried to do high fives with bank man. This celebration was not known to him, and he gave me a quizzical, worried look. Briskly he lead me back to the counter where, smiling and unburdened he handed me over to a stern looking colleague with Himmler glasses and stubbly iron grey hair. He said "NO" loudly when I asked him if he spoke French or English. "ESPANGNOLE," he declared, with great patriotic emphasis, so that all in the building would know the language he loved.

After checking my card's integrity with world central plastic control, and this took fifteen minutes, he spoke to me in excellent English. "Take this card, with this paper, and present both items to that foolish looking old man with the white hair yonder at the cash till."

The elderly bank man had heard this before. His tired eyes rolled up as they caught mine, and I joined his long, patient,

159

queue. He managed his papers and money in slow motion. When at last we met, he looked in the direction of his fun loving workmate, and held his nose tightly, as if the air around him had become too unclean to breathe. He kept the nose pose until his tormentor looked across and saw the signal, acknowledging it by a ghastful smile. I laughed loudly, and for a long time; this made those behind me fidget and fume even more — they would regard such unnecessary time wasting stage business as yet another frustration in the day.

After putting the money away, and relaxed that vélo was safe where I had left it out of sight, I looked for a venue to celebrate on the crammed sea front. We chose, there was no other, a packed café with many outside tables and chairs, under bright awnings. At the next two tables sat a German couple, and alongside them, alone, a middle-aged Frenchman. There was a three-way conversation in French, and after a few minutes, Mein Herr announced that he was off to drink in the bar, leaving his lady to their table neighbour. Mein Frau was well built, blondish, tanned and physically handsome in middle age.

Monsieur moved his chair urgently to her table, scraping it haircurlingly along the shiny, tiled floor. My café cognac arrived just after he had settled down with her. Then began a conversation which from the outset, had the clearest of themes. Monsieur referred to 'putrine', 'sein', 'vagin', 'cock' and 'orgasme'. Mine Herr was well out of earshot, having gemutlichkeit inside the café with new found friends. The sun beat down, and the Frenchman enthusiastically made his hay. It was hot stuff — a compulsive listen, which I could not have avoided, sitting where I was. I could, of course, have moved, but did not. Mein Frau was transfixed. Now and then her eyes dilated, and her breathing quickened. Monsieur had just described his activities during the past twenty-four hours in which he had conquered no fewer than seventeen times. "Oui, oui, oui," he said, "Dix-sept foix. Vraiment."

Thrice more he said, "dix-sept". She did believe him? She was in no doubt? Was she surprised that he had made love to seventeen different ladies in one day? Yes? He would explain. "Moi, j'ai un soopair cock."

160

Mein Frau, flushed, and belly dancing in her chair, considered this. Then she asked him, "Would you like to know what I think about that?"

Eyes almost on his cheeks, he leant in and put both hands on her near (left) knee. "Aaaaahhhhh, oui, oui, oh oui. Mais certainment. Tu es si belle."

The temptress looked at him, her lips now bewitchingly arranged, and she smiled like a siren.

There came from her then the sound of music to a surgeon's ear. Flatus — the most beautiful trumpet voluntaries, and compulsions ever composed. They may have been perchance, perhaps perforce, paella propulsed. Her recital was prolonged, rising and falling between three notes. All talk stopped. Eyes were on Monsieur. The Lorelei held her smile, and looked imploringly at the lover next to her. He rose, knocked over a glass, and walked angrily down the boulevard to a parked car where, shouting, he drum beat its roof maniacally with both fists. For a moment, I expected him to punish it with a tree branch. Mein Herr rejoined Mein Frau and demanded information. They spoke in German which I could not understand, but she quickly made him peaceful, and he went back to the bar for more contentment.

I was now in some pain, having had a free front row seat in this theatre of real farce. It was funnier than any scene performed in auditoria with box offices. I caught the German woman's eye. She winked at me, and I could hold myself no longer. Embarrassed, I let it go, and soon the whole terrace, when the news spread, was rocking with laughter, as shaking, we broke out tissues and handkerchiefs to mop our soaking faces. Half an hour later, I was still too weak to rejoin vélo.

When we finally did get going again, I knew that the day could be diffcult. It was likely that we would be making unscheduled stops for the sake of safe laughing. We had not even cleared the town without dismounting twice, holding myself at roadside, brought up only by the prospect of police enquiries as to my fitness to ride on public roads. Gradually, the spasms decreased, and after several hours of hard mountain work and hydration intervals, we rolled

161

down to Laredo.

From the summit of its mountain, it looked inconveniently large and crowded, so I decided that we would ride right through, and enjoy some high gear going on the flat of the town; but this was impossible. The place was choking on traffic. At one set of lights, we rested at red, alongside yet another red GB plated car. Inside were a youngish looking couple. I glanced at the male driver, and we both looked away quickly.

Evening fell on us, and as usual, I had to face the increasingly wearisome uncertainty of where to sleep and spend the night. I checked the anxiety though, by forcing myself to look forward, with pleasure, rather than dread, to the unknown: to the mysteries and surprises of the night ahead. In this much more built-up region, the hydration stops were correspondingly frequent, and at one bar around seven pm, (after Laredo) I disgraced myself.

Tired, and not concentrating well, I thought that I had been short changed. When I raised the question, I was treated to a helping of loathing and contempt. I had committed a serious social sin − impugning a local's honour. Soon the word got around, and angry, unforgiving eyes stared at me. Discomfited, and guiltily, I drained my glass in one, apologising as best I could, for the third time, and left − full of shame. Nothing more could be done, and I thought it best to leave ill alone.

We carried on, and I tried hard to believe that the mountains were now easier to take. At about nine that night we arrived at a village called Ambrosera. It comprised a few buildings, including a couple of cafés on both sides of the road. Nothing was signed HOTEL; the customary exhaustion at day's end of riding was taking charge. We went on a little longer, and then saw, built off the road and up a sharp incline, a restaurant and bar called 'LOS LEONES'. It was guarded not by lions, but by two fierce alabaster Rottweilers haunched on either side of a low wall in front of the terrace. The slope was so steep that it was hard to stabilise vélo on its stand. Around the building though, there were level patches of ground designed for a sleeping-bag, and it was this that I had in mind when I gasped a request for beer.

162

From habit, I asked if anyone behind the bar spoke French, and felt better when a young man presiding over it said, "Oui, un peu." He was a holidaying student and elder son of the owning family. I enquired if they let rooms – at the same time pre-empting disappointment by predicting aloud that even if they did, all space would be 'complet'. He confirmed this, but then, pointing to himself, said that I could have a 'chambre'. I thanked him fulsomely, and decided not to ask any more questions. We agreed that he would take me to this room (not on the restaurant premises) after closing time. I sat, cooling off on the terrace, and switched drinks from beer to port, listening to the sounds of lively talk, looking at, and thanking my shining, lucky stars.

At about midnight the son of house was ready, and wheeling vélo we crossed the N634, full of frenzied traffic, and walked along a rutty farm lane in the darkness for several hundred metres. We came to buildings, and he unlocked a barn door which is where I presumed I would sleep – on hay, and with clucking fowls. Not so. This was where vélo would be housed. I parked, and after removing wash bag and razor, we went up outside steps, and through the door of a luxuriously appointed three bedroom flat. It was tastefully stylish, being the country home of my young host's parents, who, during the busy holiday season, lived over the restaurant. I was happily surprised by such a spontaneous show of trust to a dubious looking stranger. Also, I knew that son could not have consulted father or mother when the offer was made.

The young man led me to the master bedroom, where after a long refreshing soak in the unexpected bath, I slept soundly in an enormous bed and woke with the early hot sun burning through the window glass, which I had not shuttered before sleep. There came the pungency of a strong Spanish cigarette, and I met Senor in the passageway. With grateful body language, I assured him (also with the help of snoring sounds) that I had slept deeply well. Later, his son escorted us back to the restaurant where parched, I ached for coffee. Four cups were served, and I gladly paid the four thousand peseta bill which emptied my pockets again, and created another cash flow crisis.

By now the whole family were present. Father, mother,

student son and ten-year-old brother who, even after half a dozen calls, was loath to leave his bed. He was required to meet me. They said that he was making good progress in English at school. Senor said (as younger son translated) that here was a truly international gathering – linguistically representing, and he pointed appropriately to us, Spain, France and England. They wanted to know if I would try to reach Santander that same day, aware that the ferry to Plymouth sailed only on Tuesdays and Thursdays. This was a Tuesday, but I had no intention of attempting it. Neither was I particularly bothered even about the Thursday sailing of that week. I replied that I would probably make a last overnight stay, before Santander, in the next town en route – Solares.

An hour and a half later we were there, hydrating at an outside table in the town centre. I could not have had a better seat from which to view the work of a point duty policeman who, judging by the full blooded nature of his performance, was passionately, enviably, in love with his job. From his podium, the writhing and waving maestro kept me enthralled. I did not want to miss a beat of his baton, or a ballooning of his puce, whistle happy, face. Once, instead of looking carefully at my beer glass, I was watching him, and tipped it over, but let it pass, and did not splutter about looking for sponges and cloths.

Here was a man who had dreamed of conducting all the world's great orchestras. He had mugged up on ways to avoid jet lag. He would want to arrive dynamic, and inspired, in famous concert halls all around the globe. The conductor knew that some audiences had been waiting ten years for the magic of his creative power.

This was a realist of an artist who had found peace and ecstasy from a philosophical acceptance of the invincibility of prejudice, bias, and favouritism in high places. A man who would live to see old bones, dreaming of traffic jams playfully arranged, and miraculously cleared. It was a privilege to watch him for two hours. His place on the stand was taken by an understudy who repented of the day when he took up his staff of office, and whistle. Unlike the great man, his heart, hands, eyes and feet were simply not in it, and there was nothing to stay for.

164

Chapter Fifteen

After clearing Solares, we rode on through several kilometres of flattening road at the side of beaches, and inland water stretches, and then faced another Monte Everesto. At its base, men were working on the fabric of a building, which when we got there was a restaurant. I looked in, to be greeted by Senora of printed loose frock, dyed Titian hair, glasses, and world ruler. I could see no other customers. She quickly made knife and fork signs, and the thumb to mouth jerk for drink. I nodded agreement, and unwisely let her show me to a table where the fish dish was good, but it should have been served in the shade. Moving to the dark and cooler bar area, I had some caramel pudding with coffee. I asked for the bill, paid with plastic, and saw that I had been smilingly robbed; but I decided, and not for the first time since Roscoff, that life was short (too short) to shrink it even more. Contentedly, I shirked my consumer's duty. Also, Senora, with her two sons and a daughter-in-law, had been genial. With lively body language, we had all enjoyed some good, light raillery.

Fed and poorer, we began the slow assault on the next twisting, long, high mountain. Half way up, I felt woozy and rested in a shady natural arbour off the road, listening to the screaming of brakes, and the geared rise and fall of cars, cars, and more cars. Cars with plates, cars without number.

Three hours later, I saw a modern wonder of the world. A road sign. And on the flat. 'SANTANDER FIVE KILOMETRES'. After rounding a gentle bend, there it was. The port. There were tall buildings, oil tanks, and ships. One of my road songs that day had been *Speed Your Journey* —

the Chorus of Hebrew Slaves from Verdi's *Nabucco*, and on seeing my journey's end, I sang it lustily, encoring myself over and over again, and waving irresponsibly to fellow road users.

Logic suggested that by following the seashore, we could arrive at the ferry terminal without having to find our way through the town, and so we took a right turn at the next spur. It was a bad mistake. Soon, we were boxed in with a lot of heavy oil refinery traffic, and just avoided arriving at a dead end. Turning around, I lost concentration, and started riding on the wrong side of the road. Our adventure nearly ended there and then. The driver of an oncoming petrol tanker would have been blameless if he had flattened us. We both swerved, but only just in time. Now I could see that we were on a one way spur road. I wheeled vélo back to the main artery, and the proper approach to the city; but I had convinced myself that the dual carriageway we had initially been on was an auto pista, and therefore forbidden to us. We stopped, and spent a few minutes waiting for other cyclists to show themselves, but none appeared, confirming my fear. I was wrong about this, but at the time, and in a nervous muddle, I carried vélo onto a pedestrian flyover and fought to lift the heavy load over a barrier and on to what I thought was a safe right of way. It turned out to be the original (cycle permitted) highway after all, and I was happy to be overtaken by a party of nine cyclists who clearly knew what they were doing, and where they were going.

Later, I caught up with them as they paused in an off-road area. They were members of a youth club in Dorset who had arrived after landing in St. Malo, and only three weeks in the saddle. They were in matter-of-fact mood, and seemed not to understand mine — full of pride, and sense of impossible achievement that I had got there at all: from Roscoff in fifty days. We had almost finished. Our destination (in the place that had been largely rebuilt since the fire in nineteen forty-one) was a few minutes ride away.

I left the group, and shortly after, reached the city. The road ran parallel to the harbour, and while I glanced in vain for a Brittany Ferries' sign, I did see the New Ferry Terminal display, and rode right up to the counters in the empty concourse. The whole area was deserted. Bands were not playing, crowds were not cheering, and no flags flew. I had done it. We had done it. We had travelled every inch of the way from Roscoff on our own, and the indifferent world did not applaud. I wanted ears, any ears, but there was no sign of anyone. The place was asleep, of course, because we had arrived in the middle of siesta, but well over an hour was too long to wait before I could pour out our news.

I heard the sound of Muzak coming from one end of the hangar-like booking hall, and walked vélo to a door where on the other side there was a bar. There were a few shops, and even fewer people − but people nevertheless − they would have to do. There were, at the bar, one customer and three waiters. I asked one of them, quite portly, when the Brittany Ferries office would open. He said, in passably good English, that I was too late.

"Too late?"

"Yes. Ferry boat to Plymoose sail this morning."

I knew that − it was a Tuesday, and I wanted to arrange passage for the day after next, Thursday. The man at the bar, English, fortyish, wearing shorts and dapper, told me that they would be open again at four thirty. "But they're not very helpful," he said despondently, and went on to explain that against all the short notice odds, and by single-minded tenacity, he had been able to reserve space for himself, Latin wife, baby and their bedded out truck. Only four months earlier, they had started a new life in Portugal. Things had not gone well, and they were returning to the south of England. "Yes," he sighed, "back to the poll tax, and to the council who will have to house us."

This was depressing. His sorry news was at odds with my own jubilation. I told him what I had done, and said that I had had a few adventures on the way. "Why not write a book about it," he suggested, "and then sell it for money?" He was understandably low, sore, and disillusioned. He said that he must drink up and return to the car park, where his wife and six month old baby girl would be sweltering in the heat of the day under the roof of their all purpose vehicle.

167

Befriending the bulky barman, I had some more beer, peanuts and olives. At half past four I returned to the booking hall, but not before asking this new bar tender friend to keep an eye on valiant, victorious, vélo, parked by the window. One counter position was open, and I met a happy looking blonde woman in her early thirties who had either had a good siesta, or was looking forward to a pleasant evening — or both. She had that how-good-to-come-across-you quality, and she topped up my joy level even more. We bubbled, and I all but burst. She was perfect for the part in my play that day: moreover, she spoke good French as well as English.

I gave her my open return Plymouth-Roscoff-Plymouth ticket, and she at once assumed that I wanted to book passage from Roscoff. "No, no, no," I said. "From Santander please. Please. Please." And I told her that I had ridden all the way overland.

The vélo was not in view, and she obviously thought that I had driven, not ridden, from Roscoff and was naturally unmoved and unimpressed. Her joie vanished, and sighingly, she composed her beguiling, sensual face into a solemn snapshot of grief. She spoke softly, just above a whisper — at about library level.

"You want to go to Plymouth from here by the Bretagne on Thursday?"

"Yes, please. Please. Please."

"But that is impossible. This is the middle of August, and our busiest time of the year. We already have a long, long waiting list. Without a prior reservation, there is no room in the ship."

"Even for one person and a bicycle? I am on my own."

She stood still. Her eyes and mouth opened together.

"You have come from Roscoff to Santander on your own, by bicycle?"

"Yes."

"Not by car? You have no car?"

"No, no car."

"Aah," she sang, and was merry again, showing the sort of relief we feel when medical tests have given the all clear. Her eyes danced with pleasure, the polished teeth came out to entrance once more. "Aaahh, but that's different. You're lucky. No car." She played upon her computer keyboard like a pianist possessed — her lovely light brown arms rising and falling over the notes, her gaze upon the screened sheet music.

I was joined by a father with two young children, a boy of nine, and a girl aged seven. Papa's face was kindly, he wore gold-rimmed glasses, and spoke English well. He asked me about camping and touring in the south west of England. I tried to help him, and then noticed that his Senora was resting on a seat in the waiting area. I could see the beautiful similarity between mother's and daughter's eyes. The little girl had been sung about in Gigi.

Soon the angel at the counter was ready with the ticket and the difference in fare. To avoid tempting fate I had, superstitiously, not presumed that we would accomplish our mission when ferry booking at the start. The balance owing for the Santander/Plymouth run was about sixty pounds more than the cost of Roscoff/Plymouth. Out came the plastic for another airing. Senorita and I completed our business, and I kissed her hand delightedly in gratitude.

Wishing that I knew how to tap dance, I returned trippingly to a reunion with the barman (Tubby) beaming on him, and on others within range. In a little while, the family from the booking hall came in, and insisted on buying me a glass of beer. They were from Madrid. There was a natural goodness in all their faces that urged one to know more about them, but they left before I could return the hospitality. I contemplated the value of first impressions. Were they ever both shadow and substance? Would Senor's work colleagues in Madrid, through daily association, have thought about him as I did? Would the seven-year-old enchantress have the world in her pocket, and at her feet, in a dozen years or so?

I sat alone at a corner table in the post sailing calm of the bar, well tended by the waiter who kept me steadily supplied with glasses of cold beer, peanuts and olives with stones in them. I was in a state of utter, irrational, exultant happiness in my solitude. Company of any kind would have been spoilingly unwelcome, and I sensed that Tubby and his colleagues felt and knew this. All the great barmen and women must be graduates in the psychology of mood reading. I revelled in the afterglow of our feat. I looked at vélo through the window with long, loving stares, believing that in its atoms there was a soul of some kind. The service, unabrasive atmosphere, snacks, drink and the oft recurring *Speed Your Journey* on the Muzak tape, played at a perfect level, combined to produce emotions of stupid sentimentality. Time was sent to hell. And was the Verdi wholly coincidental? I had been singing and whistling it all day long.

After a couple of hours, I snapped out of this intoxicating reverie, and knew that yet again I would hear the word 'completo' when trying to find somewhere to stay until Thursday afternoon when we would sail back to Plymouth. Reluctantly, at around seven thirty I took leave of the good bar staff at the New Ferry Terminal, and a minute's ride later joined a madding multitude in the foyer of the Hotel Bahia.

I was stupefied when I was told that there was one vacant room on a high floor that I could have for the two nights. Accommodation for vélo was harder to negotiate: there was no suitable garage. By a show of some small, inexcusable hubris, I eventually persuaded the head porter that my bicycle was a valuable, and potentially famous, vehicle. I insisted that it must be housed safely. At last the harassed and busy man shrugged, and led us to his Porter's Lodge where the Raleigh Magnum took its place among a lot of expensive luggage. Removing the things that I needed from the panniers, I carried the soiled plastic bags past the reception desk, where numerous restless people fretted, and I waited for a lift to the eighth floor. Two well dressed couples were being told that the hotel was 'completo'. I could not believe our luck. Here was a four star hotel overlooking the sea in high August, in mid-fiesta season, and we had drawn the last vacant room.

It was an en suite, twin bedded room, smartly appointed, and an ideal base from which to enjoy our triumph. Blissfully, I steeped in the complimentarily bubbled bath, gambolling in the hot water, and sang many songs, anticipating a good dinner on the premises. Life, I ruled, was the finest thing that anyone could have.

Humming and smiling radiantly, although anxious that at nine thirty pm I might have been too late for dinner, I took the lift down, and was greeted by a rather superior Cocktail Shaker in the bar. He told me that I had until eleven thirty for dinner in the restaurant. Three glasses of beer later, he grinned and served more olives, observing that I seemed to be uncommonly pleased with life. I said that he was right, and told him why. Familiar by now with the reaction of most people, I was unsurprised when even this world weary sophisticate was faithful to the line. "On your own on a bicycle from Roscoff to Santander?" The shaking of the head, then a look of true disbelief, and a possible tinge of envy. At about ten thirty, I went to table, regaled the head waiter, ate and wined well, but do not remember the fare. This was followed by deep, peaceful sleep, and room service breakfast.

It was a sultry day as I wandered around Santander on foot. At about noon I felt wooziness coming on, and so after a light lunch of gazpacho soup, slept until six pm, when I went to a massage appointment which I had arranged at a nearby clinic. The masseuse spoke perfect English, having worked in Ireland for a year as nanny to a family in Dublin. At the end of the hour's treatment I was asleep, and woke up feeling content, shrouded in a gigantic bath towel. After paying about fifteen pounds, I walked back to the hotel for another bath, happy hour, and dinner. I turned in at about eleven and slept well.

Breakfast was a frugal room service affair, after which I prepared slowly for our last short ride in Europe. The hotel bill was large, which I paid in plastic, but could not add on, through the card, a gratuity for the staff who deserved it. I had deliberately run down most of my Spanish money, and so could not express my appreciation properly. I had just enough currency for the New Ferry Terminal bar. This was explained to, and understood by, the receptionists who, I noticed, could not take their eyes off vélo as we wheeled through the foyer and out of the front entrance.

Arriving early at the ship, I returned to the bar where the staff seemed pleased to see me again, and the flow of cold beer, olives and peanuts resumed, controlled by Tubby.

171

He was busy, dashing about in bow tie, damp white shirt, and black trousers. The place was full of sweating, noisy, nervous, excited people seeing off, or being seen off. Glancing out of the window where vélo was safely in sight, I saw, seated on the terrace, a woman from the health clinic where I had been massaged the previous evening. She was sitting with a few other people at a white garden table; we smiled and waved. Shortly after, there arrived for me a tee-shirt, head band and cap, all bearing the New Ferry Terminal logo. These presents, propaganda not withstanding, made me feel foolishly important – and as there was a ready made audience, I put on all the items one by one, getting a round of seen, but unheard, applause each time. The world had turned out to cheer after all. One of the health clinician's companions worked at the ferry terminal, and made me so welcome that I was unwilling to hurry when embarkation was announced.

This was my first voyage in the comparatively new *Bretagne*, equipped with a special garage for bicycles. There was no sign of the nine cyclists from Dorset. Fifty or so machines must have been roped together when we checked in. I wished the vélo bon voyage, without feeling excessively foolish, and went to a high deck to watch our departure at two fifteen pm. Side thrusters shuddered, moorings were cast off, and we left Spain. We gathered more way, and I wondered if paths would cross with the family returning to poll tax and council.

I looked at my ticket, and saw the number of a reclining seat which I did not bother to find, knowing that when it was time, I would seek out a flat hard surface beneath a lifeless restaurant table, or in a quiet passageway, using the holdall stuffed with anorak as pillow.

As we headed through the Bay of Biscay, and there was no more land to see, and the holiday-makers settled to the voyage, I stood at the stern rail for an hour, staring at the straight, seething wake. The euphoria had escaped: the smug ecstasy was spent. Questions were asked. Had I honestly deserved a forty-eight hour break in Heaven? What was so special about this confounded ride anyway? Nothing. Could not everyone with faculties intact, and in reasonable health, do this? Of course they could. Equally, few with my limitations, would. I had been poorly prepared, untrained, and badly equipped for this self-indulgent challenge. For all that, I had faced it head on, and conquered. I left the blunt end of the ship, and walked swankily forward, knowing that nothing ever done before had given me feelings of so much self-worth.

At dinner that night, I shared a table with a family of three from Berkshire. We exchanged our news, and they told me that they had had to rush a bit from Biarritz that morning to get to the ferry on time. For them, the distance meant a few hours' nerve-racking drive. For me, it had been an arduous, perilous undertaking lasting many days. After I had said this, the man spoke. "It all depends on the way you want to travel." They were amiable people, and we chatted well.

After the trio (father, mother and teenage daughter) left, I asked the waiter for permission to smoke. He noted the empty places at the table, and said that as I was alone, there would be no objection, and brought an ashtray. I rolled up liberally, and was enjoying my craftsmanship with coffee and cognac, when I felt a hand lightly placed on my right shoulder. It belonged to a Scotsman. He was courteous, and apologetic. He told me that his wife disliked tobacco smoke, and had asked him to draw my attention to the cards on all tables in this particular restaurant requesting passengers not to smoke. "I don't give a damn," he said quietly, "and I'm sorry about this, chum, but it's the wife."

"Where is your wife?" I asked him, and he pointed to the table behind mine.

I stubbed out the cigarette, and put the unsmoked part in my pouch. Then I got up and took from the anorak, draped around an empty chair opposite, my diary and pen to write up the day's notes. I did not look at these neighbours, and sat down again in the chair with my back to them. They stopped talking, and I sensed that they were keenly interested in whatever I was doing. As I put pen to paper, I heard a female voice (it may have belonged to the wife of the gentleman who had just visited me) ask in a whisper just too loud, "What do you think he's writing?"

173

A male voice, after pause, replied in a normal speaking voice that carried easily to me, "Probably a letter of complaint to the ferry company."

He was wrong, but I felt sure that he meant well. I looked behind, caught an eye, and was in no doubt.

I went on deck, and finished the cigarette, mulling over what, if anything, could be done to help smokers and non-smokers, cyclists and motorists, serious cyclists and non-serious cyclists, to like each other a little more.